I0039029

THE
RE-EDUCATION
TO TRUE
BELIEVING

Marcus Swan

ROYAL MEDIA
& PUBLISHING

Royal Media and Publishing
Royalmediaandpublishing.com

© Copyright – 2022

All Rights Reserved. No part of this book may be reproduced,
stored in a retrieval system, or transmitted by any means
without the written permission of the author.

Cover Design and Layout: Iam Bennett

ISBN-13: 978-1-955501-15-6

Printed in the United States of America

Dedication

In dedication to the loving memory of my little brother Eddie "Rel Rel" Jackson. You are forever a part of me. May God credit to your account whatever good that may come from this book.

"When we human beings neglect to aspire to the higher realms of reality exclusive to our own nature, it nullifies one of the highlighting purposes of our being brought into existence." ~Swan

Table of Contents

Dedication iii

Introduction vii

Chapter 1 1

"The Introduction of Ideas"

Chapter 2 21

"Believing with the Heart"

Chapter 3 45

"To Believe or Not to Believe, That's the Question"

Chapter 4 57

"The Evolution of Freewill"

Chapter 5 77

"Belief in God or Faith in Religion"

Chapter 6 101

"The Ambition of a Believer"

Chapter 7 117

"Believing, the Real Social Network?"

Chapter 8 131

"Believe the Powers!"

Chapter 9   147

"I've Fallen in Belief with Someone"

Chapter 10   163

"Believing vs. Deceiving?"

Chapter 11   177

"Believing with Inspiration"

Chapter 12   187

"Consciousness Malfunction—The New
Name for Mental Health"

Introduction

This exposition can be exploited by anyone as a means to betterment of self, but for all intents and purposes, this is not a self-help book. The chief basis behind many self-help books seems to be an attempt to provide the reader a panacea for all of life's problems. Which in reality, isn't self-help at all but rather self-delusion. This type of help is impractical for two reasons: one, because there is no such thing as a magic formula capable of inactivating the trials and tribulations of life. Adversity is one of the few things in life that cannot be averted or circumvented. This further correlates with the second reason, which is the illogicalness of attempting to circumvent the very path we ourselves willingly elect to journey. This is like deliberately and meticulously choosing various foods to stack our plate with in a buffet restaurant, only to then throw it all in the trash before going and sitting down to eat. One may not have expected some of what a path comprises after choosing to journey it, but, nonetheless, we are the taker of that path. The vicissitudes of life are common to all, but we willingly choose which types of adversity we subject ourselves to by the particular paths we take in life. There are life problems we're all susceptible to, and then there's "way of life" problems everybody experiences relatively. This means the vicissitudes of the drug dealer will not be the same as those of the politician. The vicissitudes of the prostitute will differ from those of the housewife. The vicissitudes of the celebrity will contrast that of the school teacher, etc. So, the only thing left to decide after we choose our journey is the satisfaction or dissatisfaction we're left with as a result of such choices. Because in truth, everyone can pinpoint the very reasons behind the choice we make in life. What we can't seem to figure out is how those particular reasons came to be. "How do I keep inclining to do this, when I know I shouldn't?" "How do I allow myself to feel this way, when I know it's wrong?" "How do I love this person?" "How could I hate that person?" "How am I addicted to this object or this lifestyle and opposed to others?" There is no self-help book in the world that can make us averse to something we're naturally inclined to. The baffling thing about many self-help books is their outright dismissiveness of the "how's" regarding the problems people have. What good would any treatment do for the one who loves and identifies with the condition they're afflicted with. There have been countless self-help books written for those with low self-esteem, but what purpose would instructions on how to value yourself serve to one who enjoys being degraded? What could anger management do for the individual who takes pleasure in the reactions one is able to arouse through that anger? There's a difference between one's dissatisfaction with the effects brought about by our condition versus the dissatisfaction we have with the actual sickness itself. In most cases, our condition becomes unbearable only when it ceases to provide for us an anticipated effect. For example, the promiscuous woman may be indifferent to her condition of promiscuity while young and desirable. It is only later in life when she becomes undesirable for that very reason that she then considers her promiscuity an unbearable condition she must seek help for. This is also seen with the heartthrob. In his prime, the heartthrob flirts with various women to the extent of making sexually explicit comments that at the time most women find engaging, but once this same heartthrob grows a little older and a little less handsome, those same comments are construed for what they very well may be, sexual harassment. When this behavior is reported, only then does he consider his condition unbearable and deplorable. So rather than providing fruitless remedies directed at our disposition, we should first assess and tend to the predispositions that make up those conditions. And through this assessment, we'll come to find how oblivious we've been to the creation of this condition. In the advent that anyone grasps this exposition in a way that leads to self-help, it could never entail the ultimate preclusion of all of one's life problems. But it can serve as a basis by which one can begin reconciling these the incongruent concepts of life such as accountability, fatalism, evolution, reality, and spirituality.

The True Nature of "Believing" marks the beginning of what I call the science of "Naturalosophy." I define Naturalosophy as the supernatural examination into the true essence of inner natures thereby detailing its corresponding effects on modern culture. This school of thought cannot be grasped by those solely operating from a "cerebral" rationality nor by those driven by feelings and sensations, but can only be scrutinized and appreciated by individuals utilizing the optics of the intellect which I believe emanates from the spiritual heart of the human being. For this reason, the inner fruits of the spiritual heart and its being the source through which change is affected in a person are premises I rely on to further formulate many of the concepts in this exposition. So I began this introduction by acknowledging that 1) the concept of our spiritual heart being our true self and it being a supernatural instrument as well as the guiding faculty of the human being and 2) and the concept of the human being's ability, through the heart, to spiritually and intellectually evolve, are the single two premises in this book I take no claim of originating whatsoever. To these premises, I serve merely as a proponent. And to be fair, neither of these premises can really be attributed to one specific person or endemically derived from one specific time in history. These are both timeless, universal, Original ideas that have been generationally passed down and expounded upon by many esteemed individuals. Some of the highest are the great Prophet Jesus, who was quoted in the Bible (Matthew 18) as saying,

> *"But those things which proceed out of the mouth come forth from the heart, and they defile a man. For out of the heart proceed*

evil thoughts, murders, adulteries, fornications, thefts, false witness, blasphemies, these are the things which defile a man." (Mt 15: 18–21 KJV)

And the great Prophet Muhammad who conveyed through the Quran (22:46) that

"Surely it is not the eyes that grow blind, but it is the hearts which are in the breast that grow blind."

Throughout history, there've been many more philosophers, theologians, and mystics who have expounded and contributed to these two premises in their own right. I felt it necessary to emphasize this due to an episode I had. While having an associate of mine who is a Ph.D. graduate proofread this exposition for editing purposes, I was honored when I received my rough draft back riddled with terms such as, "Sources?" This was to basically imply that I needed to cite from what sources I was extracting my concepts and terms because he could not believe that I was the originator of what he was reading in this book. So, it may also come to be that professionals in this field of study such as neuroscientist, therapist, psychiatrist, and theoretician will wonder, "who is this Marcus Swan who is so audacious to construct a contemporary school of thought and what are his credentials to validate such endeavors?" So I will be the first to acknowledge that I have no societal standing that would warrant this contribution. I have no credentials that would validate my expertise in the matters I speak about. No Ph.D., no master's degree, no bachelor's degree, and no associate's degree. I operate solely from a G.E.D and the intellect I have striven to cultivate throughout my journey. The only proof I can provide of my or anyone else's ability and qualification to elaborate on the inner nature of any matter is an excerpt from the theological giant Abu Hamid al-Ghazali, perhaps one of the greatest mystics to have ever existed. In his book *The Niche of Lights*, while demonstrating the inferiority of our physical perception of sight in comparison to our rational perception of sight, he perfectly conveys the astounding capabilities of the intellect of the heart unlike any other:

> *The fourth imperfection is that the eye perceives the manifest dimension and surface of things, not their nonmanifest dimension. Or rather, it perceives their frames and forms, not their realities.*
>
> *But the rational faculty penetrates nonmanifest dimensions and mysteries of things, perceiving their realities and their spirits. It searches out their secondary cause, their deeper cause, ultimate end, and the wisdom in their existence. It discovers what a thing was created from, how it was created, why it was created and how many meanings were involved in its being brought together and compounded. It finds out on what level of existence a thing has come to dwell, what its relationship is with its Creator, and what its relationship is with the rest of His creatures. It makes many more*

discoveries which to explain would take too long, so we will cut this short.

This beautiful description concurrently outlines and provides the basis from which Naturalosophy is built. It is the intellect emanating from the heart that provides one the ability to irradiate the pretension and misimpression that both our culture and our individual selves are so steeply immersed in. The degree of one's heart runs commensurate with one's ability to see the true nature of reality. Consequently, this is not a school of thought restricted only to geniuses, Ph.D. graduates, and theoreticians as many are thought to have been in the past. But this is rather a field of thought that can be contributed to by any person who is not a victim to academic convention or intellectual complacency. For this very reason, it can especially bring about the intellectual maturation of the typical student still in grade school. The school system has done America's youth a disservice because of the withholding of the very curriculum that clarifies to them how to tap into this intellectual dimension of expression. And when I use terms such as "intellectual dimension of expression," I'm not speaking in terms of clarifying the student's view of history, clarifying how to memorize information, or clarifying how to effectively communicate in English. The intellectual dimension of expression I'm speaking in terms of is the *cultivation* of one's inner capacity to perceive inner natures. It may be true that the adeptness of these subjects further compliments one's intellect. But when the curriculum fails to develop the intellect while simultaneously developing the very byproducts of the intellect, this renders the child, in essence, a robot: a living, problem-solving, English-speaking, storage keeper of random knowledge with no guiding faculty through which to relativize these various subjects into a meaningful instrument of transcendence. Many children struggle in school, not because they're illiterate, incompetent, senseless, or attention deficient, but because they intuitively understand that the curriculum they're being taught is not meant to serve their interests. The current curriculum being taught in schools today is meant to serve society, the economy, and the overall country's interest more so than anything else. The intellect, which serves as a mere utility of the heart, has been relegated to nothing more but a cerebral learning capacity by many in the educational, medical, and psychology fields. Because society doesn't realize that in a sense, we ARE the intellect, the initiation and development of the intellect doesn't even start until one reaches college. But what does the greater majority of youth do who are not fortunate enough to attend college? This is why Naturalosophy is so imperative in today's society. This school of thought has the ability to stimulate in people the cultivation of the intellect, but more importantly the tending to of the heart. This inner dimension tended to by the Naturalosophist is capable of bringing one's nature from a state of ignobleness to one of nobility. How else would you explain somebody like Malcom X extricating himself from criminality, racism, prison, and intellectual depravity, to being someone society considered so brilliant, that despite his past, he was frequently invited to various college universities to influence the hearts of America's future leaders? As someone who spent his young adult life in the company of criminals to later becoming someone invited to visit and intermingle with kings, queens, and leaders of foreign countries?

The inner lens through which we construct what we perceive to be reality is often the factor behind much of our misconception. There are so many things in reality already obscure by nature, that if someone is also operating under a clouded perspective as well, this person is rendered perceptually hopeless. At this point, what people need most is this inner capacity to construe the intricacies of reality. Because much of our reality is constructed on a conceptual basis, it is imperative that our perspective be composed of ideas that provide one a precise impression of matters. And if one can change and augment his or her perspective, one can change and augment his or her potential. So as one sets out to analyze the true nature *of* a thing or a matter, there is no way for anybody to render such findings inadequate. Because on one hand, the physical nature of everything we see in reality is already determined and accounted for.

We cannot look at a tree and re-designate it to what we think it should be. We cannot brand a tomato as something other than what it already is. It would be illogical to speculate on the physical nature of a dog in an attempt to theorize that it could be a cat. On the other hand, the inner nature of these things and how they relate to the human being remains indeterminately inconclusive and universally open for interpretation. The Naturalosophists does not illogically theorize on what is already physically apparent but rather on the inner natures of what is not apparent. So who is there that could rebut such supernatural endeavors? The findings brought about through this school of thought do not require countless test and clinical trials to prove its validity. It does not need accreditation or endorsement from academic authorities. For this exclusive society of individuals seeking the true nature of matters, there is within their very selves a universal affirmation and substantiation of the validity of what is contributed that cannot be denied. Those guided by the heart intuitively recognize the truth of reality when they encounter it. Naturalosophy empowers any and every one able to provide a legitimate thesis into a "things true" nature. Through this thesis, one illuminates the nature of something kept obscure for the greater benefit of the whole. There are many people who partake in this school of thought without even knowing it. Sports analysts and broadcasters who speculate about the intangibles of players in key moments of the game are partaking in Naturalosophy. Economists who speculate about the fluctuation and nuances of the stock market are partaking in Naturalosophy. Political forecasters and journalists who evaluate political figures and the significant events surrounding them are in essence partaking in Naturalosophy. As human beings, we're all connected through consciousness. It just may happen that your unique contribution about a thing's true nature could provide the clarity responsible for sparking a life-changing revelation, another may desperately need to put things in proper perspective. Or it may be that your contribution enables, facilitates, inspires, or provides the foundation for another to contribute and illuminate matters that may come to effectuate change for the greater good.

This exposition is my thesis and the first official contribution to the Naturalosophy school of thought in which I have laid out the true nature of one of the most — if not the most — important tools of the human being, "Believing." This word has generally been fashioned into a concept we readily associate with power, ability, mystique, and will. But because it's used so lightly, we've all underestimated its true nature.

We have obliviously miscalculated how central a role belief plays in both the minute and significant developments that come to make up our lives. In the first chapter, I felt it necessary that I expound on the causal agent responsible for belief's viability, ideas. In this chapter, I marginally touch on the nature of ideas, their forms, what categories they belong to and how they go hand in hand with belief. This primitive breakdown is sure to be fully expounded on in later works. In chapter two, I explain how the process of believing is a product of the spiritual heart. I also outline the different operations and functions of the heart as I see it. In the third chapter, I detail the two different modes of believing, their natures, and the effects that are brought about as a result of each. In the fourth chapter, I expound on the nature of freewill, outlining how belief relates to freewill. I also expound on the concept of free nature, as well as delineating the "7 of Realities of Existence" relative to such. In chapter five, I detail how belief interacts with religion, differentiating between ideas of faith and believing. In chapter six, I explain how belief relates to ambition, explicating specifically the stages and processes through which belief brings about ambition. In chapter seven, I explain belief in its relationship to friendship. I touch on how the nature of friendships and one of the more important purposes they subtly serve for us. In chapter eight, I explain the relationship between belief and power. I explicate the nature of power and how ideas that hold power effectuate change. I also explain the role belief plays in certain power structures and elaborate on individuals who have understood the connection of belief and power and attempt to detail how they chose to utilize it. In chapter nine, I outline the true nature of falling in love with another individual, the true process one undergoes, and some of the downsides that come as a result. In chapter ten, I outline the pivotal role belief plays in the creation of deception. I slightly touch on the nature of deception and how instrumental belief is in maintaining public trust. In chapter eleven, I explain the relationship between believing and inspiration. I also outline the nature of inspiration and how our belief precipitates one's inspiration, leading to the achievement of many noble things. In chapter twelve, I explicate some of the effects of a culture overloaded with stimuli. In this chapter, I also expound on the cognitive dissonance, the problems with diagnosing, mental disorders and expound on my theory of Consciousness Malfunction. In explaining Consciousness Malfunction, I detail the "2nd of 3 R's." I also detail the nature of mental health, outlining some of its causes and effects and the role belief plays in bringing about the mental health crises and "believing" can be further used to treat many of these afflictions.

My hope is that after reading this book, we all start viewing belief as more than just an emotional conviction, but rather a noble process we're able to use for many purposes of life. It's time we realize that belief is our only means to an end. It is nothing more but our belief standing at the very center of our world, enabling or disabling us, liberating or holding us prisoner, providing us purpose and inspiration, or rendering us otiose and hopeless. The ideas we come to believe in serve as a world in itself, a world we either sustain with providential care or disregard to eventual deterioration. The way in which we exercise our belief defines our worth and is the ultimate purpose for which we were all created. I truly believe that this is the central idea behind the creation of human life.

Chapter One

"The Introduction of Ideas"

Before I could even attempt to offer an adequate exposition into the concept of "Believing," I must first provide a brief synopsis of the concept of ideas, to explain the complementary relationship that exists between the two. Generally speaking, the word "idea" has taken on numerous meanings and is used in various ways across an array of different fields. But in the immediate context, the word "idea" encompasses much more than a scientific hypothesis or an individual's personal view. Much like the nucleus apropos of an atom, ideas serve as the underlying component of any physical or intangible artifact brought about by human ingenuity. There is a process of formation for everything in creation. In human reproduction, pregnancy is first originated with the eventual evolution of an embryo into a fetus. In this instance, ideas act in that very same capacity. Ideas are the symbolic embryos of everything ultimately brought into existence. At one point in time, everything containing life was merely an idea awaiting conception into its own relative reality. From a biological standpoint, the framework of our general personality and physical disposition is already exhibited in our genetic code prior to our physical conception, which illustrates that so much of who we are is already predetermined and predesigned before our conception.

This, in effect, makes everything and everyone an idea, all with various natures and categorized into different classes but nonetheless ideas. As people we are ideas, this book is an idea, the eyes you utilize to read is an idea, and the brain located in your skull systemizing neural impulses that coordinate synapses, which facilitates our human experience are ideas. As human beings, we are capable of turning everything we see and hear into an idea. A brief description of an idea in its latent stage is pure supernatural energy. This supernatural energy is the substance from which all ideas originate in the Ideation reality, a concept that will be explained shortly. Through the belief of the human being, we're capable of converting this embryonic energy into a useable means of stimulation, thus transforming it into an idea, and possibly a subjective reality. In this state, the idea is in a developing stage much like a fetus. In this developing stage, the concentration we afford to an idea is responsible for conceiving it to maximum form. When an idea reaches its maximum potential, it's then provided nourishment through intellectual reasoning and power through emotional conviction, thus enabling it to further transfuse into our consciousness at which point it becomes an idea that we actualize into the form of an ideal, artifact, algorithm, or theory. The logic behind ideas taking the form of an ideal is that any idea that can be physically materialized into existence is also capable of being embodied characteristically. For example, an idea we internalize in relation to drugs can precipitate one becoming a drug addict, drug dealer or pharmacist. An idea relative to math, can precipitate one becoming a statistician, mathematician, or algebra teacher. An idea relative to space can cause one to become an astronaut, astronomer, or astrophysicist. But, as mentioned earlier, not all ideas are of the same form or essence and are apt to vary, depending on the category to which they belong. Ideas in their own right, have separate forms relative to their nature. The first category are original ideas, which are those that could have only originated from a higher life form prior to the existence of life. And not all cognitions are ideas (something that will be expounded in later works about ideas). Original ideas comprise the very things that either possess or sustain life and the universe as a whole. We human beings and the biological processes that sustain us are Original ideas. Subatomic particles, animals, natural resources of the Earth, the Sun, the moon, the celestial objects in the universe, and the weather are all Original ideas. Some of these ideas have been meticulously designed for a supporting purpose, while others such as the various planets within our solar system, and the countless galaxies we know to exist in our universe, seems to serve no purpose at all. In essence, anything that has existed prior to mankind or without human ingenuity is Original in nature, but what separates these particular ideas from others is that a true Original idea is transcendent in a way that cannot be re-originated. For example, it's neither possible nor necessary for human beings to originate another sun or moon. The brilliance of these transcendent ideas as constructed, are such that within their very composition, are concrete representations and designs for the production of innovative ideas we can further utilize in our relative reality. For example, though we are not equipped with the power to recreate the human anatomy due to its immense complexity, the innerworkings of the first computers were very much inspired by the way in which the human brain functions. Also, the idea of the human eye played a major role in the enhancement of the telescope, as inventors attempting to improve the quality of vision in the telescope realized the answer was to improve the telescope's angular resolution, something the human eye utilizes to facilitate the sharpness of human eyesight. Our ear drums and the way they absorb sound waves contributed to the idea of electronic radios and speakers. And the physical design of the invention of planes being originally made with wings was obviously inspired from what we saw flying in the sky, birds. Angela Chen described how even butterflies inspire ideas beneficial to humans in "Butterfly Wings Inspire a Better Way to Absorb Light in Solar Panels."

(*The Verge*, Oct. 19, 2017, https://www.theverge.com/2017/10/19/1650 3258/butterfly-wings-engineering-solar-cell-energy-biomimicry).

The wings of a butterfly have inspired a new type of solar cell that can harvest light twice as efficiently as before and could one day improve solar panels. Solar panels are usually made of thick solar cells, and are positioned at an angle to get the most amount of light from the sun as moves throughout the day. Thin film solar cells, which can be only nanometers thick, have a lot of potential. These are cheaper and lighter, but because they're less efficient, we usually use them only in watches and calculators, instead of solar panels. Scientist studied the black wings of the rose butterfly and copied the structure to create thin solar cells that are more efficient. Unlike other types of cells, these can absorb a lot of light regardless of the angle, and are also easy to make. The results were published in the journal Science Advances.... To figure out why these butterflies are so efficient, scientist led by Radwanul Siddique, a bioengineer at the California Institute of Technology, looked at wings under an electron microscope and created a 3D model of the wings' nanostructures. The wings are built from tiny scales that are covered in randomly spread holes. The holes are less than a millionth of a meter wide, helping to scatter light and helping the butterfly to absorb heat.

It was also recently published on *LiveScience.com* in an article by Ben Turner how China's exploited the idea of the Sun to create a 1 trillion dollar artificial Sun fusion reactor that was actually able to get five times hotter than the Sun. ("China's $1 Trillion 'Artificial Sun' Fusion Reactor Just Got Five Times Hotter than the Sun," https://www.livescience.com/chinas-1-trillion-artificial-sun-fusion-reactor-just-got-five-times-hotter-than-the-sun)

> *The...nuclear fusion reactor maintained a temperature of 158 million degrees Fahrenheit (70 million degrees Celsius) for 1,056 seconds, according to the Xinhua News Agency....Scientists have been trying to harness the power of nuclear fusion— the process by which stars burn—for more than 70 years. By fusing hydrogen atoms to make helium under extremely high pressures and temperatures, so-called main-sequence stars are able to convert matter into light and heat, generating enormous amounts of energy without*

producing greenhouse gases or long-lasting radioactive waste.

It can even be said that human creation was inspired from an archetype idea wherein a verse in religious scripture conveys that "God" stated, "I created man in My image." So not only do Original Ideas serve as the basis for other ideas to be created, but they also provide one a glimpse into the essence of the Divine Agent.

The second form of ideas are called Original Domestic Ideas, and these are the ideas which are innately provided to all beings alike. These are ideas that are relative and natural to the general sustainability of each living organism. Such ideas can vary depending on the nature of each being but are provided to each in a way that is naturally manifested without an originating process. We are innately programmed with the know-how to do certain things by instinct, such as parenting children, copulating, and protecting ourselves. These are ideas more relative to our physical survival, but as human beings, we are also inherently disinclined to ideas not conducive to our social sustainability as well: ideas such as mating with members of our immediate family, eating the dead body of other human beings, and killing our children. Though we have the freedom to still act on such, the social majority share a repulsiveness for such ideas. One could even assume that if such ideas were not made repulsive to our nature, it would in all likelihood lead to our social degeneration, thus segueing to our physical extinction. On a limited basis, animals are also provided these Original Domestic ideas. Many animals of the same species are in constant competition for food, mating partners and territory. In the heat of battle, one might think that animals would annihilate one another in the midst of competing for limited resources; but remarkably, there is a shared idea between animals dictating how such situations are conciliated.

According to the Encyclopedia *Volume Library* 1976, *confrontation between members of the same species are innate rituals that have been worked out over millions of years....The first stage of a confrontation over a mate or territory or social status is a threat display. The adversaries show their fangs, claws or beaks and often try to make themselves appear larger by standing upright or by erecting fur or feathers. There are various intimidating sounds—growls, snarls, roars, croaks, and squeaks. This may be enough to discourage some contestants because the square-off is intended to decide which is the stronger, more vigorous, and motivated animal. If threat does not settle matters, fighting takes place. But the weapons are not used in a lethal way. It is a pushing and shoving match or showy fencing duel between animals with rapier antlers. Venomous snakes do not use their fangs. They wrestle. Male tortoises do not attack with their beaks or claws, but instead, try to overturn their opponent.*

This and many other evolutionary behaviors can only be the product of Original Domestic ideas, instrumental to the survival of the animal species as a whole. We human beings also use this concept terrestrially as we have fashioned stop lights, street signs, and sidewalks to essentially facilitate the sustainability of transportation order.

The third form of ideas are Terrestrial Ideate Ideas. Terrestrial Ideas are usually ideas that have not been originated by human beings but yet are susceptible to being chemically or structurally advanced. In essence, the nature of these ideas are subject to our influence in a way that is unique. For example, the repugnance of human cannibalism is an Original Domestic idea not apt to alteration. Though we have the freedom to believe in or reject Original Domestic ideas, we do not have the power to influence their nature. As terrestrials, we don't have the power to change the nature of human cannibalism to anything other than what it is, repugnant—no matter how much we may try to rationalize it. However, as terrestrials we do have the power to create, dictate, and alter the nature of all Terrestrial Ideate Ideas. Our belief acts as an instrument to manipulate Terrestrial Ideas in a manner conducive to our survival, navigation, and suitability through the many vicissitudes of life in this world. Trees, water, air, and animals are terrestrial ideas that were created to be self-sufficient organisms sustaining, replenishing, and reproducing themselves, but all with natures subject to human interposition. It's only because of our ability to manipulate these terrestrial ideas that we're able to exploit trees to make paper, exploit water to create steam, and exploit animals for various purposes. And last but maybe most importantly are Terrestrial Conscious Ideas. And what makes Terrestrial Conscious Ideas so special is that of all of the ideas, these are the only ideas self-created by humans to some degree. I say to some degree because these make up the ideas through which we tend to our own existence of being. The main function of these ideas can best be described by what many psychologists have called "cognitions." So it's through this particular form of ideas that we develop all of our abstract concepts, as well as the abstract *ideas* we embody into our identity. Figuratively and theoretically speaking, I deem these cognitions to be baby ideas that are thus capable of being cultivated into teenage and adult ideas. The basis of this book and what is to follow outlines the processes of our believing in these ideas, as this multi-level process serves as the requisite causal agent to interact with and manifest ideas into fruition.

People trying to alter their circumstances imagine the way to effect change is through engaging the actual problem that appears to have brought about the circumstance, when in reality, it's the engaging of the originating idea behind the problem that brings about a real and lasting transformation. Otherwise, the same problems dressed in different variables will continually bring about similar circumstances.

Through deep introspection, one has to restructure the ideas we have internalized through belief. This is best done by considering the matters that evoke the strongest emotions in us, whether negatively or positively. This provides us an indication of which ideas are internally guiding us. The matters that stir the most intense feelings within us usually contain some type of dynamic that has either triggered or challenged our most fundamental ideas. In a sense, the ideas we come to internalize are like active entities within themselves. When these ideas are esteemed and adulated, we become inspired; when they are threatened or infringed upon, we become hostile; and when they are challenged or criticized, we become defiant. Few people actually take the time to vet what ideas they have truly come to believe in, and this would explain the unfounded, mistaken, or indifferent positions they take on various subjects. If you're ever confused as to why someone keeps making the same type of mistakes, falling into the same situations, or ending up in the same type of relationships, you should look no further than the very ideas they have come to believe in. We must all ask ourselves, how and in what way has my ideal system contributed to my success, failure, or current predicament?

When you come to unearth what your true system of ideas is on a conscious level, then and only then can you judge the merit of a given idea you've come to believe in and whether or not it's in keeping with your morals, values, and aspirations in life. The three R's, which are Remembering, Reasoning, and Ridiculing, are the keys to dismantling a destructive or unnatural idea you've invested belief in. The first R entails remembering to the best of one's ability how and why you came to believe in such an idea. And if not possible, at the very least you should attempt to recall your earliest memory of any defining moment in your past you think may have initiated the idea. Because if one can recollect the exact fashion in which the idea was originally conceived, one is in better position to adequately dispose of it. Next, you also must evaluate your family, friends, and associates to determine who else may have this same ideal system to ensure that you're no longer enabled or influenced by such mentalities. Second, you should use reason to understand the role such an idea has played in impacting the direction of your life from beginning to present. And last but most importantly, you have to make ugly the idea to yourself by reflecting on how unproductive, ineffective, and unprogressive such an idea is to you, the people you love, and the world as a whole. Anything that we deem to be disagreeable, we tend naturally to disassociate from. The more often one applies the 3 R's, the sooner one will realize that the motivating factor behind our believing in such unnatural ideas was, in effect, an act of revolt rather than principle. When one reaches this realization, restorative measures can be carried out to heal much of the damage brought about from such *inverse believing* (which will be explained in chapter 3). We are constantly looking to blame circumstances, people, our environment, and society for difficulties that we, in most cases, bring on ourselves in life. We dismiss the idea that consequence is no coincidence.

Chapter Two

"Believing with the Heart"

For many people, the act of consciously believing comes naturally, being an inherent attribute of the human heart. But in this age of social media, society is now so flooded with *visual* and *physical* stimuli that kidnap our attention, we go through life oblivious to any other realities. Speech is an innate ability of the human being, but even it has to be developed and controlled before it can be utilized effectively. This applies also to many other things we learn in our initial stages of growth such as walking, eating, writing, and in this context, believing. Many neglect to journey past the dimension of the five senses, so absorbed in our external existence that we've completely abandoned our internal dimension precluding ourselves from reaching the very tool capable of bringing about our greatest potential as human beings. Such individuals are those whose state is more oriented toward attaining fruition in the bodily and imaginary sense, rather than in a spiritual and intellectual sense. Their ignorance to the wonders of the inner heart causes them to, in some cases, stunt and impair their very capacity to believe permanently. When we human beings neglect to aspire to the higher realms of reality exclusive to our own nature, it nullifies one of the highlighting purposes of our being brought into existence. In our arrogance, we surmise that our aptitude for intelligence renders us the apple of the universe but intelligence, single-handedly, cannot be deemed the dividing factor elevating us above other creatures. There are numerous creatures throughout the animal kingdom who carry out instinctual tasks that the average human of average intelligence would find challenging. In 1976, Donald Griffin published *The Question of Animal Awareness.* The *Encyclopedia Volume Library* described it as follows:

"In that book [Griffin] defined mental experience as thinking about objects and events remote in time and space. He said that the mind has such experiences, that awareness is a set of related mental images of the flow of events, and consciousness is 'the presence of mental images, and their use by an animal to regulate its behavior.' Griffin cited a growing body of research, including the ability of a chimpanzee named Washoe to learn sign language, to support his contention that some animals carry out conceptual thinking." (The Volume Library, 1976)

So outside of intelligence, it's the power we've been given to transcend and exploit various realities of existence that truly distinguishes us from every other living organism. This unique power cannot be attributed to any type of intelligence we ourselves have acquired, but rather is a gift, wrapped as an innate product of the human heart, the same heart through which we believe—and the same heart through which we exercise our perceptive intellect.

There has always been a psychological edict that our cognitive and intellectual capacity occurs in the brain, when in principle, this is not the case. For the human being, the brain, through the nervous system, functions as a self-regulating physiological control center for the many complex purposes and processes of the human anatomy. Life within our body is not just exclusive to our state of conscious being; our corporeal human body is also an actual living organism, operating independently of our control. When we get sick due to some disease or infection attacking our body, we ourselves have absolutely no active role in our immune system releasing white blood cells to fight off these diseases. Our immune system responds to this attack on its own volition without any go-ahead or signal from us whatsoever. When we eat food throughout the day, we take no part in our body's process of breaking down this food and converting it into energy, while disposing of its excess baggage. This is a product of a digestive system operating as needed, on its own volition, without our awareness or provoking the matter. When we physically exert ourselves in various physical activities causing our bodies heat index to increase in temperature, we have no part in inducing the process of perspiration as a counter measure to excrete harmful toxins from our bloodstream and prevent the body from overheating. All of these processes are products of our peripheral nervous system. This illustrates how our physical anatomy is an actual living entity in itself. But more importantly, it shows how the processes that occur in our brain facilitates everything for the human body. The brain's nervous system is comparable to the role Washington D.C. serves for the country, acting as the sanctuary that engineers, supervises, regulates, and governs all of the biological processes that sustain the body so that we, in our true essence, are left to tend to more important realities. So the brain works with us in partnership dictating all bodily operations. Dale E. Bredesen, MD, explains this in his book, *The End of Alzheimer's:*

> *"You have a remarkably powerful computer inside your skull. It contains an estimated 100 billion neurons, each with an average of almost 10,000 connections, for nearly one quadrillion—that's 1,000,000,000,000,000—total connections, or synapses, in your wonderful brain. Every feeling, every thought, every moment, every decision, every perfectly executed arabesque, every creation, every scam ever perpetrated, every tender act, every act of terrorism, every sin, and every human kindness—all originated in these connections, which is how brain cells communicate with one another. Every thought ever thought by a human being—Pontius Pilate's decision to send Jesus to Calvary, Julius Caesar's realization that even Brutus had turned against him, the choice you made at Starbucks yesterday and in the voting booth last election day—is the result of signals traveling down one neuron,*

crossing the synapse to the next neuron in a particular circuit, traveling down this neuron, on and on until you speak or move or otherwise give real world expression to the activity inside your brain." (Avery, August 22, 2017, pp. 63–64)

These neurons in the nervous system are responsible for facilitating our ability to reason, perceive, and comprehend, and if the brain were to sustain significant damage it would otherwise impair these abilities. Neurological diseases are a very real and serious thing. The universal premise being subscribed to here is simply that the brain is not the locality projecting our awareness, reasoning, comprehension, and actual psyche, but rather the hardware that brings the above processes to fruition. Maybe because human beings have a tendency to construct things vertically, from top-down or from the bottom-up that we suppose our guiding faculty to be top oriented, when in actuality, its position is centrally oriented as wisdom would dictate. But it has been clearly established that the most essential component of any organism is usually the central component of it. For example, in astronomy we have recently learned that in the past our universe, as presently constructed, was stabilized and regulated not so much by the sun as previously supposed, but by a super-giant black hole known as Sagittarius A-Star. Researchers have found that our galaxy is actually orbiting this black hole. Events associated with this black hole, billions of years ago is a chief reason behind our galaxy being as inhabitable as it is, unlike the countless other galaxies we know to be volatile and erratic. And it's no coincidence that this giant black hole is actually located not at the top nor the bottom, but at the very center of our galaxy. Also, one must consider the positioning of the Earth's most important resource in space, the Sun. The Sun is not positioned overtop of the Earth sustaining us from above or under the Earth sustaining us from below but, due to its enormous mass, is stationed at the center of our trajectory causing the Earth to orbit it in a continuous elliptical motion.

Also in physiology, most physiologists do not consider a fetus to be viable until it acquires its heartbeat, something that emanates from the center. Another example is the ozone layer. The ozone layer is probably the most important key to Earth's ability to sustain the many dangers of the galaxy. This layer of gas surrounding the Earth acts as a protective shield, deflecting ultraviolent radiation from the Sun as well as incinerating many other harmful materials entering the Earth's surface. The cause directly responsible for this magnetic field surrounding our world is the Earth's core. Iron, heat, and the immense pressure operating not on the outside, not from the surface, but from the center of the Earth is what brings about this phenomenon.

Through technological advancement, medical research has helped us to comprehend the many functions of the human brain, mostly in a physiological sense. But because science cannot breach the nonphysical realm of human beings, science remains oblivious to the nuances of the spiritual heart, causing a misplaced notion of where our psyche is actually located. In theory, all of the ideas we come to believe in transitions through the four operations of the heart before they're brought into reality. Those four operations are 1) the operation of Spirit, 2) the operation of Intellect, 3) operation of Conviction, 4) and lastly the operation of Consciousness.

The Spirit operation of the heart is the first operation where any and every idea begins its conception. Many of the Original Domestic ideas inherent in all humans, such as the idea of a Higher Power, originate in this component. Known to many as the soul of the human being, the spirit operation serves as the nonphysical battery that powers us. Within this component of the heart is the very essence providing life to not just our personal existence, but all beings and organisms that exist as a whole. This very spirit is also what connects us to our Creator. While the intellectual operation of the heart enables us to seek and grasp the essence of the Source responsible for all existence through knowledge, it's the Spirit operation, if pure enough, that is the door through which we supernaturally are able to explore and experience the Divine Reality.

Through various forms of religious struggle one has the ability to even purify this capacity to the utmost, leading one to spiritual heights as high as the heavenly angels. This is validated through the superior states of individuals we call Prophets, Saints, and spiritual leaders, etc. Or in the alternate, through our immoral ideas and conduct, we're able to use this door to relegate ourselves to something lower than human beings, blinding ourselves to the true reality of matters. This Spirit component is the means whereby both heavenly and devilish causes are able to exert influence on the human heart. The Spirit is such a miraculous creation, it's something that can only be originated by a Higher Source. Life can in a sense be simulated through animation, as we see with machines equipped with artificial intelligence that perform jobs previously thought only capable by humans. By literal definition, the quality of life can be attributed to anything which is operative and active. The Spirit entails a much more complicated definition. If humans were to try to create a human android, as I'm sure we have, it wouldn't matter how much we designed it to look and move like a human, no matter how much human psychology we programmed it with, nor knowledge of the world, there would still be no way to impart into it a living spirit. This is the reason cloning humans is virtually impossible.

The intellectual operation (2) of the heart is the true locale of our inner perception and is actually what people are referring to when they mention the proverbial "third eye." This is the component where ideas are nourished and developed through reasoning and intelligence. And in all actuality, we could program computers to process information on a much higher level than humans ever could but a computer has to first be programmed, by human intellect, before it could carry out such functions. The heart's intellect distinguishes itself by its capacity to not just process information, but also its capacity to tend to the inner nature of things. Human beings are one of the few creatures capable of distinguishing between what is authentic and fake, genuine and disingenuous, truthful and deceptive, reality and illusion on a spiritual, conscious, ideation, and physical level. This is unique in a sense that though human beings are not the only species operating with intelligence, this quality of entertaining "realness from fakeness" is solely germane to the human experience. Sure, animals are relatively capable of projecting inconsistent impressions for purposes of hunting, self-preservation, and social status. But this specific quality is not relevant to either an animal's nature or general survival. Though it's been proven that animals share with human beings the capacity to think, it's safe to presume that animals are not beset with thoughts like "why was I created?" "Is there a Higher Power?" Or "is my romantic partner having an affair?" There will be those firmly invested in the idea that humans and animals share no fundamental differences at all, and for these individuals this may be difficult to intellectually reconcile.

But there's a much higher wisdom to be had in the idea that we human beings are the only creatures in existence, in need of such an apparatus, due to our intellectual susceptibility to catastrophes brought about from something indefinite in nature or reality. The essence of this very wisdom premises our ability to penetrate into both higher realities of the spiritual realm and the lower realities of the physical realm. Through the intellect we as a species have infiltrated and explored the aquatic world, the quantum world, the astronomical world, the physiological world, the elemental (compounds) world, the botanical world, the zoological world, etc. This same intellect also enables us to explore the higher realities of the Divine realm. But the outcome of such endeavors has throughout history been obscured to individuals dismissive of such realities. All in all, such noble aspirations as a whole are impossible for individuals not resolutely acquainted with the intellect. The intellectual operation is also home to our imagination. The imagination is meant to assist the intellect in its various functions of process including memory retention, deductive reasoning and contemplation but is now in and of itself commonly used as alternate means of perception by many.

The Conviction operation (3) of the heart is where we experience all variety of emotions. And what makes this component of the heart so important is that this is one of the means utilized to empower our ideas into existence. As   such, this component can best be compared to the extraordinary pressure needed to transform mere rocks into diamonds. This conviction works in conjunction with our intellect, providing the necessary force through which ideas are internalized into consciousness. This component also corroborates where our psyche is located, as any individual of the faintest self-awareness can accurately pinpoint the chest as being the locale from where one's emotions are radiating. For example, anyone keenly aware of the subtleties of hunger would know that there is a difference between a yearning arising from the heart for food, versus the yearning in the form of stomach pains coming as a result of the body's physical need for nourishment. This is in keeping with the phrase, "eat to your heart's content." If our psyche were located in the head as many suggest, this yearning for food we feel in the heart would actually be felt in the brain. The saying might then be, "eat to your head's content."

The fourth operation of the heart is Consciousness. Consciousness is defined by psychology as an internal mental activity of the mind, a premise obviously contrary to this exposition. In this book, consciousness is defined as "the psychical identity of a being, responsible for empowering one's reality." This component is home to both our identity and nature. It is essentially the true self of the individual. The part of man that distinguishes, I AM, just as the Source conveyed to Moses from the burning bush when questioned about It's identity. This nature giving consciousness allotted to all things with life, originates from the same Source of Consciousness responsible for bringing about all of the various realities in existence. As humans, we've been given a consciousness superior to any other in the world. Human consciousness has within it both the power to give existence to ideas and alter nature in a way that nothing else can. But there are also lesser degrees of consciousness. Each animal has a consciousness uniquely suited to its particular nature. There are instances of some animals functioning on levels similar to even human beings. In the book *Cognitive Ethology: Essays in Honor of Donald R. Griffin* edited by Peter Marler and Carolyn A. Ristau (1991), contributor and primatologist Alison Jolly reviewed research indicating consciousness in chimpanzees:

> *"...disrespect to either gorillas or orangutans (which exhibit some of the same complexities). Jolly cites various examples of social awareness deception and concealment, distraction and lying, planning ahead and creating image. Scientists are particularly interested in such behaviors because they require the animal to represent another animal's mental state. Jolly concludes that the evidence she cites shows that chimpanzees exhibit, if we readily concede consciousness in ways that human beings do, and adds, to chimps,*

it is not just because their minds are so like ours, but because their problems are so like ours."

Though there are some instances of specific animals exhibiting higher forms of functioning, animals have a limited consciousness which precludes them from the ability to access or utilize our greatest possession, belief. Because of this, they are restricted to their nature which inevitably dictates upon them the all-encompassing pursuit of their instinctual drives above anything else. For us, the human consciousness serves as the platform through which we have the freedom to elevate our original nature as homo sapiens or relegate ourselves to a state similar to that of the chimpanzee. This renders each individual's state of consciousness, a distinct self-creation. The consciousness is also distinctive in that it provides only the human a compass through which to morally navigate life, thus you have the expression "guilty conscience." When you think about the competition of life, and how we accept ideas such as survival of the fittest, collateral damage, and family planning and how such ideas are embraced by the collective, it would seem that those invested in the idea that humans and animals share no difference would more thoroughly examine this exclusive quality within humans that makes us sympathetic to the plight of fellow humans, the mistreatment of animals, and the conditions of the environment. How does one even reconcile the two? We scientifically endorse evolution as a plausibility to the extent that we teach it to children in grade school but yet we neglect the reality of this quality of moral conviction, which essentially binds us to certain practices that seem to contradict our evolutionary survival. Animals kill, steal, and ravish as an instinctual means to survival without even the slightest hint of morality or empathy for those they victimize in the process. Herbivores consume sustenance from the environment without the least bit of concern for depleting environmental resources, various animals often become fatally aggressive toward the same humans that try to help them without any remorse whatsoever and in dire situations many animals will even resort to cannibalism, some with their own offspring, all done without the least bit regret, as products of innate impulse.

> *"Animals such as rabbits and hamsters have been found to eat their own sickly, weak or dead offspring left in the nesting area in an effort to deter predators, that would be lured by the smell, from entering their domain."* (Wikipedia)

Well aware of this moral susceptibility, we oftentimes circumvent this moral quality through non-conscious means. For example, there are many judges in the judicial system who understand and acknowledge the illogical, inconsistent, and excessive sentencing guidelines that have been established. Yet, these judges have been provided the all-encompassing discretion to override many of these guidelines and do what their moral consciousness tells them they should. Unfortunately, many of these same judges ignore their consciousness and what they know to be right, using the sentencing guidelines, as an excuse to render out discriminatory and disproportionate sentences. As a society, we have created non-conscious entities to consciously bypass our very moral consciousness. We draft punitive punishments into statutory code that mechanically oversee the criminal justice system as a means to overthrow the consciousness. We create fixed surplus financial charges, tax liens, and credit fees to carry out uncompassionate reimbursement against those who cannot repay us all to overthrow the consciousness. We create health care policies and inadequate Medicaid that leaves people with medical debt, overpriced medication, and misdiagnosed illnesses, all to foster the idea that everyone has access to healthcare, as this serves as means to also overthrow our consciousness. It would seem that in such a civilized society, we would do better to heed the consciousness we've been given, rather than finding ways to render it obsolete.

The phenomenon of believing is multifaceted in that it serves as a supernatural process, an instrument, and a reaction mechanism for the human being. It's through belief that one initiates the inner dimensions of the heart. And it's only through belief that one is able to exploit each of the four operations on an independent basis. It is through belief that one tends to the spirit. It's through believing that one exercises the intellect. It's through the administration of our belief that we regulate our feelings. And it's through believing that we take full advantage of our consciousness. We are much like artists in our belief to the extent that our believing is a craft that we must first develop if one is to reach mastery. Before we can bring about transcendent endeavors, one must utilize transcendent means to do so, and believing is the means through which this is possible.

"People often speak of changing the course of destiny, taking fate into their hands, and creating their own luck, but the process of believing in our own ideas apart from those we're apportioned by circumstance is as close as one can get to this concept." ~ Swan

Chapter Three
"To Believe or Not to Believe, That's the Question"

It's virtually impossible to live a functional life without utilizing belief in some way, shape, or form. We all inadvertently exercise our belief one way or another but there's a difference between responsively exercising it and willfully exercising it with know-how. Belief itself is a natural mode of function we human beings are bound to abide by, but we've also been given the freedom to contravene this decree and thus utilize an opposite mode of this function. Thus, those who abide by the natural mode of function, exercising it in the manner intended are called Believers and those who elect to utilize the opposite side of this function are considered In-Believers, meaning those who inversely believe. Both believing and in-believing are two sides to one coin, both being similar in function but bringing about different natures. One might presume a parity exists between the two, but of the many differences, one of the biggest separating factors is reality. Belief, when used in its natural mode of function provides the believer the power to traverse realities in a manner the in-believer is precluded from. This is the real line of demarcation between all human beings: belief and in-belief or rather acceptance or rejection. You either fall into the category of employing belief for the purpose for which it was created, or using it inversely, one or the other. This, in a sense, renders us accountable on a much deeper level. Because often times, the biggest difference between people we consider to be upright or otherwise not so, is in how each exercises their belief.

When one exercises belief in its natural state, it places the believer in unity with the natural order of life, bringing one into perfect coordination with an Ultimate plan predicated by a Divine Reality. This mode of belief, exercised at its highest potential, is capable of elevating us from mere human beings to something far more superior in nature. Some might compare this capacity to metamorphosis, the natural process that animals, rocks and even plants undergo. But metamorphosis in each of these three cases is integrally brought about in conformance with the nature of each. For the animal, rock, and plant, this process is one of culmination, rather than aspiration. We human beings are the only beings capable of consciously aspiring to metamorphosis. Because of such, the believers are indispensable to any endeavor of interest and are usually the catalysts behind most of the great achievements of mankind. These types typically believe in the goodness of the world and the higher purpose inherent in all forms of life. This causes them to look for and expect the good, wanting to believe in the potential virtue of all people, situations, and things. Those naturally inclined to believe will initially stumble in the process of developing their belief, but if steadfast will always be guided to whatever is most valuable and appropriate to their nature. There is a similar Islamic principle that holds, "everyone is naturally guided to that for which they were created."

There are stories of people who have endured and survived fatal encounters and near-death experiences, by nothing more than the belief they exercised. There are stories of sports figures, entrepreneurs, and politicians who have thrived in their respective fields and credit that success to belief in an idea they've maintained over time. For example, Muhammad Ali began calling and believing himself to be "the greatest" boxer ever prior to its being universally acknowledged by others.

The people we deem morally impeccable are those who have come to believe in morally impeccable ideas; while those we deem corrupt have come to believe in correspondingly corrupt ideas. Applying belief inversely and adversely consists of not only maintaining a general state of rejection, but more particularly, a rejection in Original Domestic ideas. Original Domestic ideas are described in chapter one as the ideas all beings primordially inherit for purposes of the sustainability of existence. Through revolt, the in-believer opts to reject the validity of these ideas, choosing instead to replace and in-believe in contrasting ideas as an alternative. This takes such an individual out of the natural order of life, placing them in direct conflict with their relative reality. But the thing that makes in-belief so dangerous is that those who exercise in-belief are empowered in their internalization of these ideas, no less than the believes are. Belief is such that, even when applied inversely, still carries with it a capacity as powerful as its counterpart. The in-belief of an individual yields a force of potency equivalent to its opposite, with the only difference between the two being the energy radiated from belief being one of positivity, while in-belief one of negativity.

One would naturally assume that belief is the cause behind both good and evil ideas being brought into fruition, but this is not at all the case. Belief is by nature, a transcendent capacity. It is impossible that belief would facilitate into reality an unnatural idea, and in-belief bring about a moral one. Semantics would entail no difference between the two, but in implementation there is very much a difference. For example, as Hitler set about materializing his ideas of ethnic cleansing and world domination, it would seem that he was driven through his belief in these very ideas. But in actuality, Hitler was to a greater extent, motivated by his staunch rejection of the original domestic ideas of his time more so than anything else. So the main impetus behind Hitler's aspiration was not acceptance and belief, but rejection and in-belief. Hitler rejected his view of reality as he saw it. He rejected any idea of the religious and moral distinction he felt as associated with people who were Jewish; he rejected the status that he felt

Germanic people were relegated to; he rejected the economic system in effect during those times; and he rejected the geographical size to which Germany was consigned. Objectively, one cannot definitively say that Hitler was lacking belief in regards to his ideas. But when Hitler chose to reject the more significant Original Domestic ideas, such as religious tolerance, human equality, and social justice, he could only then be operating through in-belief, which in effect, brought about the alternate ideas of the mass extermination of Jews, the racial superiority of the Germanic people, socialism, and imperialism.

History is replete with evidence that demonstrates how anytime someone attempts to misappropriate their capacity to believe, it simultaneously degenerates both society and that individual's moral fiber in the process. The exercise of inversely believing over an extended period of time leads to a pessimistic and a negative identity of consciousness. Consequently, such individuals relegate themselves to a condition in which they're more inclined to reject ideas that denote a purpose of life, which is a very difficult state to emerge from, because while eventually these individuals may come to regret their sad state of consciousness and wish to change it, their habitual predisposition to rejection will always bring them back to the same condition, precluding their belief in counteractive ideas such as healing, forgiveness, accountability, rehabilitation, and transformation. These individuals, instead, seek to strengthen their rejection even more through the ideas they internalize, which serve as defense mechanisms. Thus pride, envy, and arrogance obscure their sense of perception, leading to self-justification of this rejection.

When these negative effects of in-believing become more and more obvious, they are met with increasing criticism and hostility from others, causing self-alienation. At this, these individuals set out to prove how everyone else is really no different in nature than they are but only concealing it instead. An example of this are those who seek out imperfections in leaders of religion, as a means to undermine the religious and the institution of religion as a whole. These types of people begin taking pride in their rejection, as though it renders them more courageous and authentic than everyone else, all the while oblivious to their hopeless delusion. Under this delusion, they squander many opportunities and prospective relationships, being solely content to share their company with others of the same nature.

These types consciously or unconsciously espouse expressions that relegate life such as "You Only Live Once" and "Live and Let Live," "Ignorance is Bliss" and "Life is a b****." When they see someone do something upright or compassionate, they presume that there must be an ulterior motive or a hidden agenda behind it. Such individuals are introverts who are distrustful, overly suspicious, and prone to doubt anything they can't rationalize with their limited level of reasoning. They're also the type that usually scorn organized religion or any type of conventional code of ethics the greater majority subscribe to. So in a sense, one can say that criminality, rebelliousness, and corruption are all indicative of in-belief. But the most distinguishable characteristic of the in-believer would have to be their obsessive endeavors to try to force reality to conform to their subjective reality.

This faulty state of consciousness is much different from those whose consciousness is in a state of malfunction (a topic that will be expounded on in chapter 12). Because those in a state of malfunction inadvertently confine themselves to a conflicted reality due to being handicapped from belief, while the in-believers willingly relegate themselves to their subjective reality as a delusional means to self-empowerment. The downfall of such individuals who try to force higher realities to conform to their lower realities is always one of implosion. The immense degree of in-belief these individuals invest into their self -constructed realities, becomes so powerful that when the gravity of a higher reality causes their reality to implode, that force simultaneously swallows the individual to the point of no return, comparable to a black hole. The reason for such implosions is because human beings are only given the ability to traverse and supplement the various realities of existence relative to our nature; however, we were not given the power to alter higher realities.

But one must not be too swift to label and categorize those who believe and in-believe as moral or immoral, because it may very well be that those in the majority who seem to be exercising this capacity with virtue, are actually in-believing in ideas not conducive to the sustainability of the collective whole of humanity; and those in the minority, who the greater part of society shuns and looks down upon, could be rightful rejecters of vitriolic ideas unknowingly bringing about the social decay of society as we know it. Social media is the main cause of the upsurge of unnatural and erosive ideas that are being streamlined right into the hearts of the masses. The average person is now exposed to so many unnatural ideas, it's becoming a struggle to repetitively reject and discard such ideas due to the sheer volume. If you can expose somebody to something long enough, eventually, they can't help but be susceptible to its exposure. Throughout history the espousal by the masses of adverse ideas has always been the catalyst behind the decline of civility, thus leading to some of the most horrific human injustices known to man.

Chapter Four

"The Evolution of Freewill"

Belief is the primary driver of predicament. Our belief provides life to our ideas, we are then able to internalize into consciousness. When an idea attains consciousness, only then can it be materialized into existence artistically as a theory, mathematically as an algorithm scientifically as a physical artifact or characteristically as an ideal we embody. In this state, this idea has now become a segment of the greater composite responsible for influencing any and all decisions we make, leading to our immediate circumstances and conditions. So, it's the ideas we invest our belief in, that eventually determine the circumstances we find ourselves in. People often speak of changing the course of destiny, taking fate into their own hands, and creating their own luck, but the process of believing in our own ideas apart from those we're apportioned by circumstance is as close as one can get to this concept. By forgoing the opportunity to build an independent ideal system, absent external influences, one practically vacates their "God" given freewill. When we encounter any idea, we have the choice to either believe or reject that idea. To essentially give it life or keep it non-existent. The only other option is to delay the choice for further analysis, but there is essentially no other option in this process. Believing with the intellect is the most sophisticated method of exercising this capacity, which begins with us initially deliberating how compatible an idea is with what we already believe. Through the intellect, one first imagines what the internalization of this idea would mean for us and who we would become by it. One should allow the idea to settle within our very heart, ascertaining the behavior, sentiments and attitudes that derive from it to determine whether these are in conformance with our most important objectives in life. After conceptualizing this idea, if we find it to be compatible with our personal nature, one then moves to internalization. This entails internalizing the idea into our consciousness through emotional attachment or conviction. Internalization is brought about through the charging of the idea with both intellectual and emotional energy. Energy generated from the intellect comes about through nourishing the idea with various forms of thinking. The energy generated from emotions stems from our most potent feelings. This is why some of the most significant changes in people's lives come on the heels of a significant emotional development that affects them. Very few realize that within our most intense emotions lies the source of our greatest strength. All of these powerful feelings act as potential sparkplugs capable of providing the necessary energy needed to convert ideas into consciousness. It is the combination of the two that brings about the internalization. Once an idea attains consciousness, we are then able to bring all of its latent potential to fruition through our very own nature.

As humans we are nothing more in essence but a sum of what we truly believe; a walking, talking, assemblage of ideas. Everything that we do, say, or think—every choice, preference, and inclination—relates directly back to our inherent ideal system. If you look at the environment one occupies, their status in society, the reputation they hold, the type of people they surround themselves with or lack thereof, and the overall quality of their life, you could somewhat determine how a person has utilized their belief in the past, or at present. We tend to dismiss minute details about people's choices and mannerisms chalking it up to genetic and biological factors, never realizing that every little detail about anything a person does, serves as an insight into that person's deeper truth, or in this instance, their ideal system. An ideal system, as used in this book, is defined as a construction of ideas a person assimilates into their consciousness which come to make up one's essential identity. We assume that we're the sole overseer of our affairs and that the choices we make are autonomously independent of any other influences, but in actuality, it's our ideas that serve as our metaphorical board of trustees, inducing every decision and path we choose in life. Most of us essentially adopt the ideal system of the people we look to for imitation during adolescence. So in most cases, there is a matriarch or a specific member within either our immediate or extended family whose ideas and manner of belief are both consciously and unconsciously adopted as custom by the rest of the family. So from the onset of our development we become somewhat a victim of circumstance, involuntarily adopting the disposition of our predecessors, and the longer we preserve in these ideas, the more we compromise our prospective individuality in the process. And in the cases where one manages to somehow circumvent this pattern, one's family, culture and society criticizes them for deviating off course, impelling them to immediately return to the fold. Ironically, in America, we pride ourselves on being the land of the free, but the truth is the greater majority of us are intellectually, emotionally, and spiritually subjugated to the prevailing norms of those we most closely identify with. So how free can you really be if you're mechanically conditioned as to how and what to believe? True freedom lies in the ability to fashion oneself however one sees fit, rather than becoming a product to a set of social conventions, relative to a particular background or upbringing. How can any of us afford to do away with such an inalienable human right as the ability to be who we truly wish to be, rather than what we're conditioned to be? Freedom is the ability to choose our own path rather than being forcefully ushered down the path we're assigned to, all of which are direct products of the ideas we invest our belief in.

The lack of appreciation we have for the concept of freewill has caused us to relegate this idea to something only exclusive to human beings. WordWeb dictionary defines freewill as the power to make free choices unconstrained by external agencies. But by this same standard, one could also argue that animals have freewill. Though they may lack the same degree of intelligence, they are endowed with a discretion relative to their particular nature, which enables them to unconstrainedly move and act at their own will. When you apply this same standard to any particular organism, everything has freewill. Everything that has a nature is given the power to act within the relative basis of that nature. So if freewill is seen in limited proportion to each organism's nature, we could attribute freewill to every organism in existence. But if this proposition has merit, it could thus not apply to the human being, due to the ability we have to either elevate or relegate our intrinsic nature. Consequently, freewill, by definition, is an inadequate description for the human aptitude to dictate its own affairs. But the more appropriate term to denote this quality would be freenature. Our freenature finds its true perfection, not through our mere unconstrained discretion of experiential actions, which is something even animals share in, but through our potential to unconstrainedly transcend the various experiential realities. And before one can further understand the nature of freenature, one has to first apprehend the true nature of the realities of existence.

Existence can be separated into different divisions of reality. For us as human beings, reality is categorized into "The Reality," Spiritual reality, Astronomical reality, Ideation reality, Subjective reality, Terrestrial reality, Conscious reality, and Unconscious reality. "The Reality" is the highest and Truest form of any and all realities of existence. In essence, it is the only Reality and true basis of all existence. The other realities that exist are mere offshoots and products of its "Reality." This reality is a Divine Reality, home to all heavenly bodies and sources of causes. It is the only Reality with its own Consciousness as was demonstrated in biblical scripture when It identified Itself as I AM. This Reality is one very few of us have knowledge of due to the deficiency of our physical nature. Because of the Transcendence of this Reality, not even Prophets, who are the most acquainted with This Reality, have been able to provide a detailed and sensible account of its interior affairs. There have been rare individuals, comparable to spiritual explorers such as saints, mystics, and sages, who have purified their hearts to such a degree that they were permitted spiritual access to this reality, but because of Its Majestic nature, that access has always been miniscule, sometimes even ruining the sanity of the explorer in the process. The little we do know about this reality can be attributed to Divinely inspired scripture, which throughout history has been humanly altered and exploited many times over. But even through the remnants of revision there still lies some reality to be had from these altered scriptures in circulation today. And for those genuinely curious about the nature of "This Reality," while unbeknown to many, there happens to exist a single Divinely inspired scripture, still in the original state in which it was inspired. But the finding of such a reliable chain of transmission would require a comprehensive study of the history of all three Abrahamic religious scriptures, something very few have the desire, patience, tolerance, or objectivity to do.

Next is the Spiritual reality. And this reality has no physical realm but is purely spiritual in essence, capable of being occupied solely through the state of one's heart. This reality has mainly been occupied by rare spiritual leaders from the past, whom we call Prophets. These certain individuals have been commissioned by a Higher Power to fulfill a specific mission to the world. And because of the gravity of this noble purpose, such individuals can only be of the highest nature, enabling them unrestricted access to this magnificent reality. This reality holds many secrets of existence that would afford typical humans undue prominence. The knowledge in this reality surpasses all forms of phenomena knowledge in existence. This is the reason Prophets were always some of the most followed individuals in the world, regardless of their economic status. So consequently this reality is deliberately reserved for only the purest of individuals. Though there are individuals such as clairvoyants, diviners, fortune tellers, psychics, and mediums who have somehow managed to snip knowledge and information from this reality, the means through which these individuals are capable of accessing this reality are inconclusive.

The next reality is the Astronomical reality, which testifies to the Majesty of a Higher Power, like nothing else can. This may also be the reason that the astronomical reality is situated as a symbolic buffer between "The Reality" and the reality we human beings are physically stationed to. It's possible that the "Reality," knowing man's propensity to explore and exploit foreign realms, created this reality for no other reason but to be a boundary which signifies man's trespassing into a Private Reality. Consequently, this reality was not made conducive to human survival. Though humans have provisionally managed to physically explore this reality, conditions relative to gravity, frigid temperatures and oxygen shortage all preclude the human from fully occupying this reality, keeping much of its mystique hidden. This astronomical reality consists of realms such as planetology, time, physics, distance, energy, and extraterrestrial lifeforms. We've also acquired much knowledge from this reality, such as the ability to predict the weather, history, astrology, and relativity. The intellectual exploration of this reality has also produced rare individuals such as

Albert Einstein, Isaac Newton, Stephen Hawking and Chandra Prescod-Weinstein.

Next are the stages of reality relative to consciousness. The first of which is the Ideation reality. And this is one of the highest realities of human functioning because it involves a conscious exercise of belief as explained in this exposition. Because this reality is subject to our belief, it is constantly changing and evolving as a result of our ideas being impressed upon it. It is through this reality that human civilization was established, as ideas that have come to make up ethics, procedures, laws, and governments are given a platform through which to be materialized. It is also in the ideation reality that original domestic ideas, we innately inherit from "The Reality," are able to serve their intended purposes. This reality is exclusive to human beings and serves as a realm through which we collaborate, share, and mutually exchange common ideas. This reality enables humans to identify with one another on a much more intricate level than other conscious beings are able to do. The greater majority of people merely inhabit this reality sporadically or in mere presence, but do not permanently occupy this reality due to their abandonment of the inner heart, relegating their nature to that of mere animals. This also explains why animals are precluded from this reality, as their nature limits their ability to participate in the realm of ideas. This is not to imply that animals are completely void of ideas, but limited. The real reason we don't hold animals criminally responsible for their actions, is not because they're oblivious to their doings, but because we unconsciously recognize their preclusion from this communal reality of ours. This also explains why we don't hold the criminally insane legally accountable as well.

Next is our Subjective reality. The subjective reality is generally initiated by human imagination. This reality makes up an individual's pure idiosyncratic impression of existence, brought about through the inverse exercise of the intellect. The in-believers who insulate themselves in this reality are those who either refuse to acknowledge and develop their inner dimension of self or those who superficially construct their realities to suit their preferences. Such individuals are those who disdain much of what they see in the higher realities, to the extent that they opt to occupy a made-up reality rather than partake in any of the real ones. This further leads to the In-belief of many ideas that negatively impacts one's identity and brings about a distorted subjective reality. It is in this reality that individuals attempt to isolate themselves from other realities through subjective realms of virtual reality, cyber realities, euphoric realities, and intoxicated realities.

The next reality of existence is the Terrestrial reality. And within this reality exists the many realms that make up life on Earth. The terrestrial reality is also our physical reality, as it serves as the corporeal and graphical framework for all terrestrial life. Within this reality are realms of zoology, biology, geology, phytology, and the aquatic realm. All of these are independent earthly realities, subject to human exploration and interposition. Human activity has greatly affected many of these realms, sometimes to the point of extinction. This reality provides all organisms a shared unified field of perception, sensation, and vibration. This reality is home to physical interactions with lesser terrestrial beings. Because we humans are able to occupy this reality, we have the ability to interact and interfere with the development of non-human organisms such as the planting and cultivating of vegetation, manufacturing raw materials from the Earth, and chemically manipulating compounds. The reason we cannot interact with the deceased, demons, and spirits is because they don't share in this same reality. For those invested in the belief in the idea of evolution, our primate ancestors would have been limited to this reality.

Next comes the Conscious reality. Aside from our physical experience, this reality is made up of humans and animals. Artificial intelligence is limited in its ability to partake in this reality because of its lack of consciousness. The reason that we can have limited interactions with other beings that possess consciousness and have them respond to that interaction is because both occupy this same reality.

And lastly is our Unconscious reality. In this reality, the human being seems to occupy a higher state of consciousness than normal and seems to be afforded a greater access to higher realities than usual, but due to our inability to simultaneously occupy both the conscious and unconscious reality, we're precluded from exploring the possibilities of the unconscious reality. There are instances throughout our day to day affairs where we unknowingly occupy this reality, often as a result of our doing something habitually but in all such experiences we're like unconscious robots until abruptly something brings us back to conscious reality. These are usually brief episodes but in rare cases they may last for extended periods of time. There has always been a mystique about the unconscious reality and there may even be rare individuals able to draw from this reality but the means through which this is possible remains a mystery. This reality is occupied by individuals in the advanced stages of Alzheimer's, or those who are brain dead, in a coma, or simply sleeping.

This brief synopsis of the active realities in existence was essential to further demonstrate the true nature of freewill and freenature. The freewill of each living organism is limited to conform to their relative nature. And the relative nature of each organism dictates what reality they occupy. As previously stated, our flexible nature gives us the unique ability to elevate or relegate ourselves, thus enabling us to transcend to higher realities of existence or descend into lower realities. So essentially, our free nature is our ability to incline to higher natures of being or lower natures of being. For individuals whose nature solely dictates upon them the indulgence of carnal pleasures, the border of their free nature will generally not exceed past the terrestrial reality. Those whose nature is dictated by imagination will not exceed past subjective reality. The individual whose nature enjoins on them the assiduous study of a particular science will usually not exceed past the ideation reality, while the individual with the purest of natures will not be precluded from any of these realities, enabled to traverse at will, which in essence is free nature at its peak.

"Before one could ever access the majesty of "The Reality" in the spiritual realm, one would first have to pursue and recognize "The Reality's" majesty in the physical realm." ~ Swan

Chapter Five

"Belief in God or Faith in Religion"

In Webster's Dictionary, the term [name] has various definitions. The first is, "A word or words by which an entity is designated and set apart from others. The second is, "A word or words used to evaluate or describe, often disparagingly." And the third is a "Representation or repute as opposed to reality." As we approach the subject of religion, it's extremely relevant to the understanding of this exposition that "God" be identified in the most coherent way possible. As these three definitions would illustrate, the name "God," as well as any other name, fails to adequately express the nature of this Extraterrestrial Entity. Judging by the standard set forth in the first definition, the name "God" does not in any unique way set apart this Entity from all else. If we use the second definition for a standard, it also falls short in describing or capturing this

Entity's true essence. The third definition is also an insufficient label for "God" due to its capacity to be used as a title or epithet which denotes human aptitude. The inadequacy of the name "God" or any other term attributed to this Entity is demonstrated in its variation across religious, ethnic, and cultural lines. "God" is the name we use in English, "Yahweh" in Hebrew, "Dios" in Spanish, "Jehovah" to some, and Allah in "Arabic." For this very reason, many people equate these variances in name to mean a plethora of deities, when that is not at all the case. So from this point forward, the *expression* that will be used to refer to this "Extraterrestrial Entity" in this book will be "The Reality." I believe "The Reality" is the most relevant term because it best explains the only type of interaction and relationship we can have with such an "Entity." As time continues on, it seems that we human beings are drifting further and further away from the true sense of Reality. Throughout history, our awareness of true Reality has run commensurate with our duration of existence in it. Meaning, the closer we were to the beginning, the closer we were to the true essence of It. And the further we drift into time, the further we're drifting from it. This could only explain why each generation of human beings seems to be more morally inferior than the one preceding it. For purposes of this book, I won't attempt to journey any further. The aforementioned along with the presumption that this expression will prove most helpful in elucidating many of the important points in this exposition is why I chose it.

From a spiritual standpoint, one can say that matters of human belief are the sole purpose for the creation of life. This is demonstrated by the fact that belief, or the lack thereof, is the main theme for the world's three major religions. In Christianity, the Prophet Jesus speaks obsessively about faith in the Bible, alluding to the notion that if one's belief or faith is strong enough in "The

Reality," anyone could do the very same miracles that he himself performed. The line of demarcation which qualifies someone as an actual adherent to any religion, is one's belief. By Christian standards, a person is not deemed a true Christian unless one "believes" either that Jesus was "The Reality" incarnate or that Jesus was the begotten son of "The Reality." In Islam, Muslims are referred to in the Quran as "believers." The Prophet Muhammad conveys the idea that belief in "The Reality" goes hand in hand with one's worship, which is central in the life of Muslims. It's universally understood that in order to be considered an orthodox Muslim, one has to "believe" in the monotheism of The Reality, which is a belief in the absolute Oneness of "The Reality" without any partners and that Muhammad ibn Abdullah was sent as a Prophet by "The Reality." Anybody with a belief contrary to this is not acknowledged as an adherent of Islam in the traditional sense. In Judaism, the belief is that the covenant "The

Reality" made with the Jews is still active and that they're still to this very day "The Reality's Chosen People." But unlike Christians, many traditional Jews "believe" that Jesus has yet to return.

The fact that "The Reality" has placed such an emphasis on faith in all three Abrahamic religions, demonstrates how powerful the concept of belief really is. To some degree, all three religions concede that in the afterlife or on the day of judgment when one stands before "The Reality" to be held accountable, the verdict of recompense or condemnation will be on the basis of one's belief. This notion alone offers a small glimpse into both the marvels of the human spirit as well as the generous nature of "The Reality." The detail with which "The Reality" has created the heart, invisible to the naked eye, yet revealing itself in everything a person does, bears witness to the Transcendence of "The Reality." When you think of how intricate life is as well as the immensity of outer space, in comparison to something as minuscule as the mere belief or in-belief of human beings, the notion that "The Reality" would create all of the former for the sake of entertaining the latter, demonstrates the immeasurable love and worth He has invested in mankind. But more importantly, it signifies the true significance of the heart, which is the exclusive apparatus we use to both believe and in-believe. There is no conceivable way to practice any of these three major religions without some application of belief. And if one attempted to do so, one would render futile his endeavors on all three religious accounts. But even if the idea of "The Reality" was proven to be a fraud, produced by a secret society of the wealthy to control the masses, as some may surmise, essentially, this still would render religion no less conducive to the well-being of the human consciousness. The belief in the idea of a judgment day, in which after death we will stand before "The Reality" to be questioned about our actions, provides many people a strong incentive to maintain at least some sense of decency. This idea alone leaves the human being hesitant to completely abandon one's morality for nothing more but precaution. The explanation offered to us about life and death through religion, serves as the moral crutch we need as human beings from the dread of the unknown. The idea of not knowing what awaits us after death is a distressing and humbling admonisher of how weak and helpless we really are, and thus brings us face to face with the reality of how grave and uncertain our futures are because of it.

Not only is the unknown agonizing for us, it's utterly terrifying. Every night you go to sleep comfortably, believing that tomorrow will undoubtedly bring another interval of daylight. The belief we have in this certainty is so strong, it prompts us to preplan our affairs not just for tomorrow, but for days, months and even years on in. But imagine if you were to wake up one day at approximately 10:30 a.m., after getting a full night's rest, and walk outside, expecting to see the morning sky, and you are met with the stillness of the night. Imagine the feelings you would get waking up to what should be early morning daylight and seeing the sky just as dark as it was before you went to sleep. You would immediately begin checking your watch and clocks to see if they were functional, turning on your television to see what the news and media were saying about the incident, telling yourself that you must not have slept for as long as you thought, making phone calls to loved ones for clarity. But once you realized you were not mistaken and that the situation was real, you could then do nothing but attempt to rationalize it, attributing it to things like a solar eclipse, global warming, or judgment day. And when this process of rationalization failed to relieve your confusion, your state of mind would eventually deteriorate to one of outright trepidation. This one situation would invalidate everything you thought you knew, weakening your ideal system and the sense of security you had in your understanding. In attempts to soothe the pain of not knowing, man has always postulated, rationalized, or speculated the unknown, even prior to having the scientific evidence or reasoning to support such attempts. Throughout history, physical evidence has never been the calling card of belief. We have always utilized our belief to placate our inherent vulnerabilities. For example, the universe, with all of its cosmological instability, poses endless perils consequential for life here on Earth. Yet, it's nothing more but our belief providing us the emotional and intellectual security to live indifferently to these countless jeopardies continuously staring us in the face. Without such, would otherwise cause us to be consumed by distress. So belief in a Higher Power is all the more in line with a well-balanced sense of sanity because as previously mentioned, the mere idea of not knowing will not suffice the heart of the human being.

For many, religion serves as the exclusive apparatus capable of enabling one's spiritual happiness. But there is a difference between spiritual happiness and happiness that stems from the ego. The happiness of the ego comes about when one's identity, whether inflated or not, is validated. Happiness of the ego is fragile and temporary, needing to be constantly validated. While spiritual happiness is much more stable, providing one a sense of peace and lasting fulfillment. It comes as a result of maintaining one's purity and not having anything taint the soul. That and other religious or mystical practices are meant to elevate the state of the human spirit. But essentially, the key to understanding both forms of happiness, is in the belief we invest into ideas relative to each. Whether it be morally or superficially, there are numerous ideas derived from religion that create the necessary basis to pursue both forms of happiness. For example, Christianity offers people the idea of eternal salvation prior to the coming of judgment day. The essence of this idea is that if one believes in their heart that Jesus Christ is the Son of The Reality and that He was sent to the world to die for the sins of humanity, such a person is saved from judgment and will have eternal life in paradise. This idea is so powerful in essence, its internalization brings about relief, hope, and assurance, by removing any and all spiritual anxiety, plaguing those who are uncertain of what awaits them. So in a sense, this liberates the Christian from the guilt and remorse of indiscretions, because of the idea that Jesus paid the price and redeemed them from sin. This idea serves as a defense mechanism enabling Christians to maneuver through life as if they have spiritual immunity, as opposed to adherents of other religions who obsess about the state of their souls. With this impediment of spiritual accountability removed, unadulterated happiness becomes the objective. And this pursuit of happiness usually comes at the expense of worship because if the job has already been completed, what purpose is there to work? There are many preachers, missionaries, and evangelists who are now teaching Christianity in terms of prosperity and happiness. The Prophet Jesus states in a biblical verse that, "I came so that you may have life and have it more abundantly." This verse has been used to corroborate ideas of happiness, prosperity, and fulfillment. The New Testament, now being the secondary source to the bible gives everyone leave, through the Holy Spirit, to work out their own salvation, through fear and trembling. This gives anyone the right to interpret, clarify, identify, and rationalize what Jesus's intent was behind saying such things. So the majority of people now are either claiming to be happy, doing the things that make them happy or in desperate pursuit of happiness. But to be objective, in spite of the mass internalization of such ideas, there are controverting forces challenging many ideas of orthodox Christianity. Like everything else, Christianity is not a monolithic religion. There are various sects within the religion of Christianity with their own distinct view and application of the teachings of Jesus.

There are also many ideas being falsely exploited within the religion of Islam that offer some Muslims the opportunity to indulge in unlawful practices with a less than usual remorse. This is to in no way cast aspersion on the religion of Islam itself, but only to demonstrate how belief can be mis-utilized in the pursuit of one's personal interest. Unlike Christians, Muslims do not endorse the idea of premature salvation. In Islam, the idea is that Hell is something that everyone, at the very least, will traverse through and whether you safely pass through or fall into it is contingent on one's worship, actions, and quality of the soul. So, for the Muslim, the purpose of life is not the pursuit of happiness but rather the pursuit and accumulation of good deeds that would render one safe on the day of judgment. But there is an established belief in Islam that the Prophet Muhammad will be granted intercession on the Day of Judgment and will use that intercession to implore The Reality to remove many Muslims from Hell until finally all are removed. So in the idea that this benefit is only exclusive to Muslims, there are those who, dare I say, feel more inclined to carry out certain practices contrary to the pursuit of paradise, for the lone reason of believing that Hell for them would only be for a duration rather than eternity. There are also individuals whom society deems extremists, who exploit ideas of Islam to justify their endeavors.

In the initial stages of Islam, when Muhammad first began propagating his message, he was met with harsh and malevolent resistance from the people of his region. He and his followers were vilified, berated, and assaulted for practicing this newfound religion. This went on for a while as

"The Reality" forbade Muhammad and the Muslims from any type of retaliation or violence. During this non-violent stage, there was a handful of Muslims who were killed for refusing to renounce Islam and abandon Muhammad. It was during this trying time that "The Reality" revealed a verse in the Quran wherein it was stated

"And consider not those that were slain in the way of God to be dead. Rather they are alive, nourished in the presence of their Lord, all rejoicing."

This triggered the beginning of the Islamic principle that, Martyrs do not experience death in the same way everyone else does but are granted in exchange a much more lenient form of it. And from this point on, martyrdom was thus exploited by some Muslims with ambitious intent rather than the spiritual consolation it was intended to be. This is the very reason that those considered extremists are so eager to fight and die for what they deem to be jihad.

"The root word for Jihad is Jahoda which means to endeavor, strive, struggle, exhaust. The noun Juhd means the making of one's utmost effort and to struggle to achieve one's object. From this root word Jihad is the Quranic terminology for struggle and it means investing one's capabilities and resources by the utmost striving-including fighting in order to obey God's commands and to seek His pleasure and to establish His Din." (From Quranic Keywords *by Abdur Rashid Siddiqui)*

Where the problem arises is when certain Muslims deem any and every issue a matter of jihad worthy of murder and martyrdom, when not every issue qualifies as such under Islamic law. As the case with Christianity, such principles of Islam are not exploited by all Muslims alike. There are Muslims within the religion of Islam who condemn such malpractices of the religion.

As is the case with both Christianity and Islam, there's also those in the Jewish religion who falsely exploit the Mosaic law practiced in Judaism, which prescribes that a sacrifice be offered in "atonement for" certain sins committed. As in other religions, there are some Jews who are more disposed to committing unlawful practices, with the intention of afterward compensating financially through atonement. This is clearly not "The Reality's" intent behind the construction of this concept. The misinterpretation of this concept conveys a false implication that one has a license to do anything outside of the law, as long as one atones for it afterward. As is the case with the other two religions, there are also contravening sects within Judaism that oppose such an idea, along with many other principles of orthodox Judaism.

The actual process of believing in The Unseen Reality is an act of conscious will, rather than mere supposition. There are many who stake claim to the belief in "The Reality" in theory, but not in actual practice. To believe in the existence of "The Reality", in mere theory, is just the same as believing in the existence of air, germs, electricity, or minerals. One knows these things exist through our benefiting from them but as long as they're serving our purpose, we give them little to no thought outside of that. This is merely affirming a thing's existence for purposes of defining reality, rather than believing in an idea for the purpose of actualizing it into reality. This is not to relegate "The Reality" to the level of just an idea, for this would be impossible. "The Reality" is the Source of all ideas and could thus not be an idea because It was not created by anything nor can It be further perfected by anything. But we human beings experience life through the prism of ideas, so the only way to initially expose ourselves to "The Reality" on a personal level, is through first internalizing the idea that "The Reality" is not just an idea but an actual reality that exists and that all other realities emanate from It. So the act of *willfully* believing in the idea of "The Reality's" existence rather than just believing in theory, is essentially an endeavor to occupy this "Reality." But because "The Reality" is veiled through invisibility, we have no choice but to utilize our supernatural capacity of belief to aspire to it. Though "The Reality" conceals Its majesty from visual perception. It's essence is all the more manifested through the wonders of Its ideas. The enormous size and extreme hotness of the Sun, the vastness and extreme conditions of space, the immense radiation and solar energy emanating from celestial objects, and the incalculable galaxies we know to exist outside of our Milky Way all testify to the Majesty and Power of "The Reality." The human anatomy with all of the intricate processes and meticulous detail in which it was created to operate; the cohesion and order through which nature functions assigning to everything in wildlife its measure, ration and balance; and the processes through which the Earth sustains itself facilitating the existence of life when all other planets in our solar system fail to do so adequately all testify to the Knowledge and Wisdom of "The Reality." The idea that the universe is continually expanding, the laws of physics, quantum physics, and astrodynamics; the speed at which light travels from great distances in spaces; the concept that the colossal mass of black holes creates space-time ripples; and the statistical calculations of the actual age of our universe, all testify to the Transcendence and Timelessness of "The Reality." These marvels all correspond directly to the nature of our belief, enabling us to grasp some essence of "The Reality" without physically seeing It. This begs the question of why we human beings have always attempted to reify "The Reality" through evidence that does not correspond to our belief. The nature of our belief does not correspond to supernatural, metaphysical, or extraterrestrial miracles brought about terrestrially. This demonstrates itself many times over through stories in the bible that describe various Prophets who exercised miracles to prove to the people that they come in the name of "The Reality." In the majority of such cases, the people still did not believe in spite of these miracles, even to the extent of killing some of the Prophets as a result of their disbelief. The reason was because the nature of these miracles did not correspond to the nature of the people's belief, so without understanding the inner nature of things, these people could not bring themselves to accept faith. Or, in other words, their inability to believe was brought about by an inability to rationalize miracles which did not conform to their human understanding. Before one could ever access the majesty of "The Reality" in the spiritual realm, one would first have to pursue and recognize "The Reality's" majesty in the physical realm. Which brings us back to the concept of believing in the existence of "The Reality" through the practice of conscious will, rather than mere theory. This act of believing in the existence of "The Reality" is something that must be developed and perfected before it can be fully appreciated. The act of believing in a Higher Power itself need not be explained, being natural and relative to all human beings. But such an endeavor is extremely difficult because of the distractions that arise as a result of concentrating all of one's belief on a single idea as powerful as the existence of "The Reality." Throughout the course of a day we routinely invest our belief into so many things unknowingly, making it problematic to solely concentrate our belief on the existence of "The Reality" without having it interrupted. But if one is able to overcome the many obstacles latent in such a task, the outcome can be life changing, elevating one to *higher states of consciousness.* When one sets out to willfully believe in the idea of the existence of "The Reality," it naturally prompts one to seek more and more knowledge about "The Reality." Because as one endeavors to aspire to higher realities, a requisite degree of knowledge into how to go about this is first necessary, otherwise its conception is obscured. As knowledge of "The Reality" can only be provided by "The Reality", this natural compulsion for knowledge about "The Realities" arises in the human being as a result of willful believing, along with the necessary course of conduct needed to guide the collective to the accomplishment of this objective, thereby validating the institution of religion and The existence of "The Reality" itself.

"When one's aspiration is internalized into consciousness, ambition is born, at which point our motivation system is enabled to do its bidding. At this stage, one's nature, motivation, and aspiration are all working in concert toward a common objective." ~ Swan

Chapter Six
"The Ambition of a Believer"

This particular concept of belief is not the abstract idea associated with miracles and supernatural occurrences. This is not to negate such approaches to belief, but the methodology offered here is more pragmatic in nature. In this instant, belief is approached as a verb, being an action or a process one carries out to reach an intended result. The definition for belief presented here is "an immaterial process, utilized by human beings to materialize both physical and metaphysical phenomena into existence." Or put differently, "an internal process one utilizes to give life to what has yet to be created." As it stands, it is "The Reality" alone with the exclusive power to give existence to life, but we human beings are graciously afforded the power to give life to ideas. It's impossible to relocate an idea from the incorporeal world to the corporeal one, without first pushing it through the birth canal of belief.

Our belief serves as the conduit for any and all ideas brought into fruition for the human being. The spirit giving life to our body is neighbor to the same capacity through which we exercise belief. This essence through which we believe, has yet to be physically identified or quantified, being immaterial in element, but serves as the central locality of true life for the human being. As the heart is the underlying battlefield where antagonisms are truly won or lost, one's belief and accompanying ideas are an army on one hand, fighting against one's in-belief and rejection on the other. Success or failure, happiness or misery, peace or chaos are all products of this very war; the manifestation of these into reality merely serve as a secondary cause of its outcome. The right degree of belief in a particular idea can usher someone down a path of life full of turmoil and misery or of happiness and success. It's safe to say that if one examines every individual who has attained any degree of success or eminence, or in the alternative, those who've placed themselves on the wrong side of history through nefarious, immoral, or corrupt acts, it will all result back to how those individuals exercised their belief.

There has always been this idea that our ability to reason is what distinguishes human beings from animals but this cannot be determined definitively. There are some animals found to carry out activities requiring levels of intelligence comparable to humans. So in reality, it's not so much our capacity for intelligence that makes us unique, but rather our capacity to believe; and through that belief transcend to higher realities. If animals had this same capacity the elephant, gazelle, and zebra might aspire to be omnivores and thus the hunter, rather than the hunted but without it, animals are precluded from aspiring to higher natures or higher realities. In this context, our belief gives us the ability to manipulate our nature to bring about the conditions we so desire rather than our conditions confining us to our very nature.

When something becomes a part of one's nature, one naturally acts in conformity therewith. Our natural impulses and inclinations are a direct product of the nature we occupy. Whatever we are composed of internally will ultimately be manifested externally. And the reason is because, as human beings, we've been inherently furnished with motivation systems that involuntarily compel us toward objectives that sustain our survival. For example, regardless of how much an individual becomes accustomed to exquisite foods, a long enough period of starvation will compel that same individual to abandon those preferences and consume the coarsest of foods with the utmost pleasure. The wisdom behind such a system correlates to the susceptibility we humans have to eradicate ourselves. Had we not been created with a natural impulse to eat, human beings, in the heat of other pursuits, would likely neglect to sufficiently nourish ourselves and perish. Had we not been created with the impulse for sex, we would fail to procreate in a manner conducive to our survival and likewise perish. Had we not been created with an impulse to learn and understand, we would become indistinguishable from animals and eventually facilitate our own demise. This motivation system serves to fulfill the Original Domestic ideas that preserve our existence but it also simultaneously functions in direct correlation with our determination, if utilized intellectually. This makes the motivation system even more profound because it's not just limited to compelling us toward our carnal impulses. This motivation system also compels us toward our personal objectives, which in this case would be our *ambitions.* An example is the individuals we label as pedophiles. No one is outright born a pedophile. This state is reached from a progression of steps.

We see the concept of ambition, as well as the people we judge to be ambitious as mere wells of selfish greed. When in reality, ambition is a much more complicated process than one of mere aspiration. One who is aspirational is often impulsive and goes about achieving such aims in a much more artless fashion, while those who attain to ambition are more calculated and meticulous. Most of the desires one is subjected to are externally produced, not in a sense that we generate them ourselves but rather they generate and present themselves to us. Ambition on the other hand takes months or maybe even years of our willingly inclining to a particular desire, which is often rare. Before this process of ambition is fully complete, it usually happens that one is confronted with an intervening predicament as a result of such an aspiration. When such a predicament arises, this relative calamity limits or precludes one from actively indulging in it directly, while the ambition itself, still resides in one's consciousness. We see this with many retired professional athletes, police officers, and ex-drug dealers who love to reminisce and gloat about their glory years. But if during this process, this intervening predicament never occurs, this further allows the individual to continue indulging in the aspiration until a state of ambition is fully realized.

Individuals who become ambitious are facilitated to this state through factors that are conducive to one's experiences in an almost natural way. Ambition in its preliminary stage, is best defined as a desire turned aspiration. We all have ideas of desire that come and go with little to no impact on our consciousness, but it isn't until we give this desire the requisite amount of attention, that it develops into an aspiration reaching maximum form. Once an aspiration, the power we furnish it through lust and rationalization leads to its internalization, at which point it becomes something much stronger, essentially overwhelming one's focus above any and everything else, thus ambition. But in essence, the manner of converting a mere desire into an ambition is a long and arduous process. It entails first that one identifies with the principle idea of the desire on a personal level. This involves an individual's idiosyncratic perception of such an idea, in combination with the context through which it is deemed to have impacted one's past, regardless of whether the experiences were positive or negative. This intimate conception of the desire provides one the basis to justify subjectively empowering it into reality. This is a subjective identification usually facilitated through one's imagination, so most likely it will not be apt to rational interpretation. But why most of us feel the need to justify our aspirations is the bigger mystery. It seems an almost inalienable necessity for humans to rationalize any and every act we carry out, whether the rationalization comes before or after the act. If one were to ask some of the most ambitious individuals what is the impetus behind their exerting efforts of attainment, one would probably hear the most noble, awe inspiring, and heartbreaking validations imaginable, but in most cases, gratification of some type is usually the core driving force behind most human endeavors of aspiration. Our inherent need to rationalize and justify our actions, speaks to a higher purpose and a deeper, more Extraterrestrial accountability we're subject to.

At this point, our aspiration is like a cancerous cell, consuming any and everything it encounters for no other purpose than a means to grow in potency.

In essence, the aspiration has now taken on a life of its own, consuming any sustenance available to it; This includes everything one experiences in the environment one occupies, such as music, movies, books, or through interaction with concurring individuals, no matter how unsound such nourishment is. It is after the continuous consumption of all this sustenance, that internalization transforms the aspiration into ambition. When one's aspiration is internalized into consciousness, ambition is born, at which point our motivation system is enabled to do its bidding.

At this stage, one's nature, motivation, and aspiration are all working in concert toward a common objective. For example, let's take a typical teenager from the inner city who entertains the idea of selling drugs. 1) This individual starts off identifying with the desire to become a drug dealer through circumstance. One is usually born in such an environment that propagates such a lifestyle. In such situations, it's highly likely that either this individual's mother or father or both are either addicted to drugs or alcohol, actively involved in the drug trade or have been in the past, or have been incarcerated for offenses relative to such. So subjectively, this individual doesn't adopt the social stigma of crime and selling drugs the same way the average person might. But due to such an environment and one's experiences, one rather sees the drug dealer and a life of crime in a glowing fashion. The typical teenager in low-income environments is constantly confronted with the idea of drug dealing, seeing the nice cars of the drug dealer, the expensive clothing, the beautiful women one is with, the power one has, the cohorts who seem to be loyal to the drug dealer. Because of all this stimuli, the teenager is constantly contemplating the idea of selling (1. Providing the attention, the idea needs). This is a perception very few can understand or identify with. This same individual who was born into these circumstances is usually socially handicapped because of it. Because these type of environments and circumstances more often than not breed poverty, single parent households, unfit living conditions, lack of education, and low self-esteem, it's safe to assume that these individuals might feel that the fruits of selling drugs would empower and even liberate them from such drawbacks. So one very easily develops an affinity for the drug dealer and the fruits of a life of crime (2. Providing the emotional attachment). This causes this individual to now bring this desire into realization. At this point, everything in the individual's life is now a source for strengthening the potency of this aspiration, until ultimately it becomes the only reality the individual defiantly acknowledges. Mundane affairs of life—such as the preference of music one chooses to listen to—have now become for the individual something much deeper. One's choice of music is now chosen for motivation, becoming somewhat of a battle cry for this very aspiration that reinforces its validity. One's choice of romantic companions is no longer what they once were but is now a reflection and product of this aspiration. One's friends and associates are now also mere reflections and products of such an aspiration. At this point, the aspiration is bordering on internalization, if not already. In the midst of such undertakings, one is often threatened with misfortunes due to the true substance of the aspiration. But by this time this individual's lifestyle is so oriented toward the indulgence and attainment of this aspiration, it's impossible and impractical to invalidate its merit. If the individual continues in such a state, avoiding the many tribulations and obstacles naturally associated with such, it enables one to nourish it more and more, which then leads it to the attainment of consciousness, becoming a component of one's essential nature almost permanently. This process of desire turned aspiration, turned ambition is a common occurrence in our society although unbeknown to many and encompasses not just the one aspiring to sell drugs. This can also be applied to those with aspirations of playing professional sports, being a stock broker, selling real estate, becoming a doctor, or merely being a trophy wife. Our ignorance of the power of belief and in-belief, and the role it plays in solidifying our desires into ambitions, has rendered people almost powerless to their immediate or imminent conditions. How many times have we shrugged off the drug dealers' premise of how addictive selling drugs can be? How many times have we seen professional athletes attempt a comeback later in their careers? How many times have we seen people in relationships go from one relationship to another, yet this person's choices of partners all seem to have similar characteristics? So is it that much of a wonder why each relationship inevitably ends the same, causing them the same heartbreak? Is it that much of a wonder why these people continue to fall for the same type of individual over and over again? The process of recovering after one has internalized the wrong desire can be excruciating. When that same desire becomes an ambition, the hope of recovery is almost impossible.

So to summarize this process of ambition, it begins with an idea in the form of a desire. When one conceives of such a desire, continually contemplating it, it is eventually able to mature into an aspiration. One then internalizes this aspiration through rationalization and emotional attachment. If the internalization is successful, this aspiration attains consciousness, at which point it becomes an ambition, we idealize into our nature. When and if this happens, these individuals reach such a state that they begin to consciously or impulsively place themselves in situations that lead to the eventual direct or indirect commission of such acts. So in a sense, the actual act serves as a secondary cause to the first, which would be the process of internalizing such an erroneous desire from onset. This is where the real evil is committed. The actual byproduct of the internalization is just a secondary cause that can be justified, mitigated, or concealed.

"The measure of potency for any idea lies in its equivalent ability to either advance, alter or unduly preserve the present social order of the time." ~ Swan

Chapter Seven

"Believing, the Real Social Network?"

As human beings, we have a natural tendency to bond with individuals we deem similar in nature. From the beginning of time, people have integrated under the basis of common identity, as those on each continent confederated with the occupants of its own territory forming laws, governments and then territorial designated nation states. After most of the major governments were established on each continent, this process of amalgamating continued. But as time went on, the idea of common identity was later expanded, also including common interest. This resulted in countries forming government coalitions across continental lines, then throughout the world. The advent of World War I demonstrates how these ties of allegiance were then constructed:

> *The major allied power... were Great Britain..., France, and the Russian Empire.... Other countries that had been,*

or came to be, allied by treaty to one or more of those powers were also called Allies: Portugal and Japan by treaty with Britain; Italy by the Treaty of London of April 26, 1915.... [The] United States after its entry on April 6, 1917." ("Allied Powers: International Alliance," The Editors of Encyclopaedia Britannica, https://www.britannica.com/topic/Allied-Powers-international-alliance)

The opposing countries consisted of Austria-Hungary, Bulgaria, Germany, and Turkey. By the time of the Second World War, the chief allied powers were Great Britain, France, Canada, Poland, Yugoslavia, the Soviet Union, the United States, and China.

More generally, the allies included all the wartime members of Unites Nations, the signatories to the Declaration of the United Nations." (Allied Powers: International Alliance, The Editors of Encyclopaedia Britannica revised and updated by Jeff Wallenfeldt, https://www.britannica.com/topic/Allied-Powers-international-alliance#ref754272)

And on the opposite end of the spectrum were the Axis of powers of alliance, which included Bulgaria, Germany, Hungary, Italy, Japan, and Romania.

World War I was a byproduct of European imperialism, as various countries with expansionary ideas secured alliances in preparation for what seemed to be an unavoidable clash of interest. After the conclusion of the war, many countries—having lost more than gained—were left feeling humiliated and bitter. Many citizens, being nationalist, were left mortified by what they deemed defeat and began calling for major changes to government. This, in turn, prompted many governments to begin refueling resources for more warfare that would come in the future. This may be one of the reasons that during this time many countries became more oppressive and tyrannical than ever before, as political ideas such as socialism posited by Karl Marx and Nazism by Adolf Hitler began to take root throughout

Europe. Adolf Hitler's rise to power in Germany was probably the defining moment in the 19th century, in large part because of the rate at which his ideas were being espoused and internalized by the masses, in Germany in particular. Ideas such as those outlined in his book *My Struggle* (*Mein Kampf*) entail that the integrity and honor of Germany could only be brought about through military victory in Europe. He also decreed that the nomadic or Germanic people were a superior race, and that it was their destiny to rule mankind. The empowerment of Hitler set in motion a series of occurrences which would later lead to World War II. The culmination of World War II would end in what Winston Churchill would call an "Iron Curtain" being assembled in Europe, with one half of the continent inclining toward ideological ideas of democracy and the other half communism. This would also usher in a new era where alliances were established on shared political and economic ideas above anything else: shared ideas such as democracy or autocracy, capitalism or socialism, religious policy or separation of church and state. And up until now, it is these very ideas that forge the basis of all the current global alliances such as the North Atlantic Treaty Organization (NATO), the European Union (EU), the League of Arab States (more commonly known as "the Arab league"), or the Organization of the Petroleum Exporting Countries (OPEC), etc. This further demonstrates how we as a people, generally ally ourselves with those who believe in the same ideas we do or at least the most pivotal ones. This is really not a phenomenon in itself, as all relationships are cultivated on harmony. The more concordance people have with one another, the better the chances are the relationship will grow. Harmony cannot take root in the midst of continuous divergence, regardless of how trivial the issues are. Even in situations where the relationship is not ideal but there exists an understanding, there has to at least be some common ground to maintain continuity, otherwise friction will segue into fraction.

This might cause one to ask, is it not true that opposites attract? Or, is it not possible to have friendships with people we have absolutely nothing in common with? The answer is, in theory, no, but in practice, yes, to some extent. For the sake of peace, tolerance, and mutual collaboration, yes, we can absolutely bear and even sometimes enjoy the company of individuals we share nothing in common with. Yes, it's absolutely possible to care about the well-being of someone we cannot identify with, as long as the most significant ideas separating us never come into conflict. An example of this was seen with the Colin Kaepernick situation in the National Football League. Colin Kaepernick, a former high profile NFL football player began protesting police brutality by refusing to stand during the performance of the National Anthem before games. After months of this going unnoticed, someone eventually took notice and people began criticizing him and accusing him of being unpatriotic and disrespectful to the veterans who served in armed forces. To demonstrate his loyalty and to convey that the gesture was not one of disrespect but rather one of social protest against racial injustice, he lightened his approach by kneeling during the anthem rather than sitting. This gesture quickly became a social movement, prompting others throughout the sports world to likewise kneel during the anthem in protest. Colin Kaepernick's public scrutiny and subsequently being blackballed from the NFL only stirred more NFL players to protest in support. This put the NFL, fans, and many of the NFL owners at odds with players who protested, as ratings begin to drop as a result. The NFL found itself caught in the middle of a firestorm, as this issue affected many African Americans, a group that makes up more than 85% of the NFL, and its economic bottom line, as fans fervently opposed to such a gesture, threatened to boycott the NFL. Dallas Cowboys owner Jerry Jones, one of the more respected NFL owners, and a billionaire from Texas with conservative political views, did not agree with Kaepernick's gesture, making a formal statement to such an effect that such a protest would not be tolerated from any player in a Dallas Cowboy jersey. Jerry Jones later lightened his stance on this issue attempting to promote solidarity with his players but never wavered from the idea that players should stand during the anthem. The issues and conflicts created from the protest of Kaepernick would have never occurred had Kaepernick not expressed his personal ideas. Such a situation also illustrates how we're all socially entangled with various individuals we have nothing in common with; People with ideas directly opposed to ours, and it's not until these opposing ideas come into direct conflict, that we discover who our true alliances and friends really are.

Anyone that has ever had a confidant, a best friend or an intimate companion has utilized belief. Many would like to believe that the feeling of a connection with another human being comes about naturally, unexpectedly and, inadvertently, but a connection between two people is first and foremost an idea that one has to believe in. There's a difference between the congeniality and goodwill we experience from a stranger, during a brief interaction in passing, as opposed to the connection we feel toward someone we consider to be a close friend. The reason being is the connection we feel with our close friends is, in actuality; an idea we believe in of a connection we have with them. The stronger the belief of both individuals in this common idea, the stronger the friendship will be. But friendship itself is unique in that, there are certain people we encounter in life whose mere presence brings us out of our *imaginary state of mind,* into our actual state of believing. There are many people, who without a causal agent, are not equipped to methodically utilize their power of belief. Or, in some cases, both individuals stand ill-equipped to initiate a state of belief independently, only able to do so through the interaction with the other. These individuals thus attach themselves to anyone able to inspire in them a state of temporary belief. This can only be possible through the vulnerability we expose ourselves to with people we deem close friends, rendering us subject to their influence. The more time we spend interacting with our friends, the more we mimic their state of heart. In every friendship there is a balance to be found; there is an admired and an admirer, a beloved and a lover, an inspirer and an inspired. The state of the former will always dominate that of the latter. Then there are rare individuals whose belief is so powerful and infectious; it naturally elevates others to a similar state, without their being aware of it. People such as Martin Luther King Jr, Lyndon Johnson, Mother Teresa, and Barrack Obama are examples. Such individuals not only inspire in us this state of heart, but also through their day-to-day affairs, illuminates to us how to exercise our belief in a way most beneficial.

There are many individuals who, through their unwillingness to tend to their inner dimension, apt to settle for the lesser state of belief offered through friendship. Because the path to abstaining from external pleasure for purposes of aspiring to higher states of inner self is one of unpleasantness, loneliness, and self-reflection; this is a path many refuse to journey. This is the reason friendships are so cherished in our culture. Anyone who's ever had a friend understands the fulfillment one receives by talking, laughing, listening, and intermingling with them. When our spirits are down and we're feeling low, there's a reason we seek out our friends first. There's a reason our friends are usually the people we effusively unmask our souls to. There's a reason that our social reality is one of great importance, specifically during our most important years of development.

All of this can be associated with the heart and the exercise of belief our friendships engender in us. And if it so happens that these friendships no longer provided us the ability to believe, this marks the beginning of the end of that friendship, after which we would then seek another to fulfill this same purpose. It wouldn't matter if we met someone who believed in all of the same ideas we did, if for whatever reason, that individual did not inspire in us a presence of heart through which to believe, a friendship would only be inconsequential.

In the WordWeb dictionary the definition of ethics follows as, "the principles of right and wrong that are *accepted* by an individual or a social group." In Webster's II, third edition, ethics is defined as "the study of the general nature of morals and specific moral choices an individual makes in relating to others," and also "A system of moral principles and values." In the Black's law dictionary 9th edition, the definition for ethical is "Of or relating to moral obligations that one person owes another; esp., in law, of or relating to legal ethics."

In each definition there are two common factors relative to ethics. 1) All three definitions imply that ethics is a recognized system of code and 2) All three describe ethics to be a social phenomenon requiring interrelation with other individuals. This means that ethics can be thought of as a unified body of ideas that must be acknowledged and shared by a collective group of individuals. Consequently, whatever ethics we come to believe in serves as our initiation into a community of countless other people exercising these same ideas. So in a sense, ethics is subtly used as a means of social incorporation. Is this not the reason that ethics is separated, relative to each specific field? There is business ethics, human resource ethics, legal ethics, workplace ethics, social ethics, etc. The reason that social media's become the phenomenon it has is due to the ideas we share being more comparable than ever before. Our shared ideas provide us all a measure of common identity.

Chapter Eight
"Believe the Powers!"

Our capacity to believe is the single most powerful feature of the human creation. So by virtue of its power, we're responsible for employing it with the utmost caution and consideration otherwise the effects could be detrimental to self and society as a whole. Some of the most heinous and atrocious acts known to man, originated with nothing more but an unwavering belief in an erroneous idea. Every idea that we internalize, has within it a potential potency to effect change. The measure of potency for any idea lies in its equivalent ability to either advance, alter or unduly preserve the present social order of the time. For example, the universal idea that incest is immorally wrong, socially decaying, and a biological health hazard can be considered a potent idea held by the greater part of society. It's generally believed that it's in the best interest of the majority to maintain this idea in a way that is conventional for all. One would judge the potential potency of this idea by the effect it would have if this idea were *inversely believed* in by the majority. If by chance, there emerged an individual or group of individuals, who were staunch proponents of incest being legitimate and legal, individuals who possessed a strong enough degree of belief in this idea, the intelligence to substantiate it, and the charisma to audaciously challenge the status quo in a way that would also prompt others in society to begin questioning it. What would that do to our societal order, our values, our world? The impact of such an idea, applied inversely, would no doubt alter the social order of society. But one need not conjure up hypotheticals to corroborate such a truth. We've had countless movements in the past as well as the present significantly impact our society, which initially started out for some as merely utopian ideas of what could be. Ideas such as the legitimacy of homosexuality. Objectively, the idea of homosexuality has not always been considered legitimate to accept. There was a time in the past, when much like incest, homosexuality was an idea the greater majority in America found abhorrent. Same-sex marriage was not only considered shameful and desecrating; it was constitutionally illegal. But as of recently, statistics confirm that,

Americans [are moving] dramatically toward acceptance of homosexuality finds [General Social Society (GSS)] report. Although sharply divided, public attitudes toward gays and lesbians are rapidly changing to reflect greater acceptance, with younger generations leading the way, research by NORC at the University of Chicago shows.

In addition to a plurality who now approve of same-sex marriage, Americans overwhelming support basic civil liberties and freedom of expression for gays and lesbians, in contrast to sharp division on such issues in the 1970s. Taken together, the results show a clear 'trend toward

greater tolerance regarding homosexuality,' said Tom W. Smith, director of the General Social Survey at NORC and author of the NORC report, "Public Attitudes Toward Homosexuality."

The rise in support for same-sex marriage has been especially dramatic over the last two decades. It went from 11 percent approval in 1988 to 46 percent in 2010, compared to 40 percent who were opposed, producing a narrow plurality in favor for the first time. ("Americans Move Dramatically Toward Acceptance of Homosexuality Finds GSS Report," NORC at the University of Chicago, news release, accessible here.)

Any time there's a new idea forced or trying to be forced into the consciousness of society, there is always a leading catalyst or catalysts behind such endeavors.

Evelyn Hooker, a brave psychologist at University of California, Los Angeles (UCLA), began undoing this belief [abnormality of homosexuality] in the early 1950s. A gay former student told her,

"Evelyn, it is your scientific duty to study men like me." Hooker agreed, "He's right—we know nothing about them." When she told the psychiatry department chair she wanted to study normal homosexuals, he replied, "there is no such person!"

It may seem to younger generations that many of the fundamental rights we enjoy today have always existed due to the fairness characteristic of their nature but social campaigns such as the civil rights movement, the feminist movement, and the equal opportunity movement have all originally stemmed from ideas people have invested a substantial belief in, to the extent that these ideas were then brought into existence, thus changing the social climate in the process. Power is the only means through which ordinary individuals are able to impact the social landscape of the times, and our sole means to effectuating such power is through the belief we exercise. Yes, believing is power.

Some of the definitions of "power" given by the Word web dictionary are, "the possession of controlling influence" or "the possession of the qualities required to do something or get something done." Nowhere is the exercise of power more evident than in politics. A politician's pursuit of power begins in the preliminary stages of campaigning as endeavors are made to discredit, outwit, and relegate their opponents, while simultaneously elevating and ingratiating themselves to the public for purposes of being elected to public office. If successful, one is then sworn into office and afforded the ability and responsibility of exercising various powers of government. But one cannot achieve such aspirations without acquiring a formal vote of confidence or (belief) from the greater part of the public. So in a sense, a politician's first exercise of power is acquisition of the public's belief. The very staple of politics as a whole, is the ability to secure the belief of as many people possible. This is a quality that, in reality, affords the politician a degree of influence, absent the occupation of government office. As a society, we seem to have no reservations about investing our belief into politicians, regardless of their inconsistencies and contradictions. It seems that the unrestricted access of information we have regarding their affairs creates somewhat of a connection and impression of familiarity to them. Information such as their past history, cultural background, achievements, failures, likes, and dislikes all allows us to determine if such individuals are worthy to be the very embodiment of our political ideas. One may think that we honor politicians for their ability to lead, adeptness of communication, or personal integrity, but in actuality the reason we hold politicians in such high regard is due to their serving as mediums through which our personal ideas are voiced and implemented apropos of the affairs of government. The process of electing someone to government office who purports to be majority representative superficially validates the notion that everyone's voice is heard and that the people are controlling the government rather than vice versa. But under this umbrella of political guise, some of the shrewdest politicians are able to dupe their voting bases into believing that their political motivations are strictly in keeping with voters' ideas and interests, while in reality the intentions behind much of their actions are meant to serve their own selfish interest instead. A classic example of such a politician would be former President George W. Bush regarding the invasions of Afghanistan and Iraq. And then there are the politicians who utilize power, through the belief they procure to accumulate more power such as Mitch McConnell. Mitch McConnell is a politician who has managed to procure the belief of his respective voting base as well the belief of his fellow politicians in a way very few have in the history of politics. McConnell's illustrious political accolades include

U.S. Senator, Chairman of National Senatorial Committee, Majority whip in the 108th[h] Congress, and he has been both Minority leader and Majority leader in the Senate. It can also be said that, in all but the first 13 senate races McConnell has run for in Kentucky, the margins he's won by on average have been respectable. McConnell's statesmanship, along with his ability to intimately identify which ideas voters in his state are most invested in, has been the foundation of his sustained success, which in a state with the history Kentucky has, is not particularly difficult to unriddle. This would explain why McConnell's most spirited and brash expression of such ideas would come during the presidency of Barack Obama.

For what it is worth, McConnell identifies with the ideas and values of a former Republican party no longer in existence. Though McConnell has cultivated a connection with his bloc, the information provided through Wikipedia entails that McConnell cannot educationally or economically identify with most of his loyal voters. McConnell is actually from the city of Louisville, not from the rural counties of Kentucky that make up his bloc. McConnell, who is college educated, attended both University of Louisville and Kentucky University, as opposed to many of those in his respective voting. McConnell, who is not a product of poverty and who in 2021 is reported to have a net worth of $35 million dollars, cannot identify with voters, many of whom are poverty-stricken with little income; and McConnell who in the initial stages of his career was not a hardcore conservative but a moderate Republican. McConnell was so moderate a Republican that in his early years, he attended many democratic civil rights rallies including the 1963 March on Washington for jobs and freedom, where Martin Luther King delivered his "I Have a Dream speech."

It seems that at an early stage in his career, McConnell must have come to understand what he needed to do and who he needed to be to extend his political career out of Kentucky and into Washington. As mentioned earlier, most politicians become puppets in their aspirations to embody the ideas of those they represent wavering back and forth in attempts to placate voters. McConnell becoming aware of this inevitability at a very early age has brilliantly managed to assess a plethora of ideas motivating the hearts of people and exploited those ideas to sustain his political longevity, making him one of the few who have, to some degree, used the political profession to serve his purpose rather than allowing himself to be chewed up and spit out like so many others.

In the context of exploiting the belief of one's voters, it may reasonably seem to some that Trump was in fact more masterful of this than even McConnell. But the distinguishing factor between the two is the political aptitude of one above the other. While Trump is just limited to capitalizing on the radical ideas of the voter, McConnell's ability to exploit the belief of others for his own personal interest is not just limited to the popular vote, but encompasses even the belief of his fellow Republican senators as well. McConnell has had the bizarre ability to unify members of the Republican party in a way that serves his own personal interests more so than anyone else's. It might seem odd to some that someone who has been a U.S. Senator since 1984 has never once opted to run for United States President. One might foolishly attribute this to a lack of ambition, but McConnell has opted to direct his ambition to a state of relevance, in the long term rather than the enjoyment of relevance in the short term, understanding that in reality, the presidency is a short-lived experience. He is probably the only Republican minority leader in the history of the Senate with no presidential aspirations, which as a result gives him an aura of someone with no ulterior motives, just someone with the best interest of the party at heart. To fellow Republicans with less experience, less status, and greater aspirations, McConnell is seen as an indispensable ally, and an almost kingmaker light. This idea of being somewhat of a kingmaker or a "king breaker" is the source of McConnell's greatest power, making him the authority on what direction the Republican party will take in the Senate bringing about cohesion and uniformity.

> *"In today's Senate, McConnell can decide virtually by himself what the chamber will do—and even what it will consider doing. You may have first noticed McConnell early in 2016 when he proclaimed the Senate would not consider any nominee appointed by President Obama to fill the Supreme Court seat vacated by the death of Antonin Scalia. McConnell made this announcement on his own, within hours of Scalia's death."*

("How Does 1 Man Have So Much Power Without Being President?" Ron Elving, August 17, 2019, National Public Radio, accessible at https://www.npr.org/2019/08/17/7518 36584/how-does-1-man-have-so-much-power-without-being-president)

According to Purdue University political scientist Bert A. Rockman, *"Pure party line voting has been evident now for some time...but rarely has the tactic of 'oppositionism' been so boldly stated as McConnell did."* ("The Obama Presidency: Hope, Change, and Reality," Social Science Quarterly. 93 (5):1065–1080.   doi:10.1111/j.1540-6237.2012.00921.x. ISSN 0038-4941)

According to University of Texas legal scholar Sanford Levinson, *"McConnell learned that obstruction and Republican unity were optimal ways to ensure Republican gains in upcoming elections."* (Levinson, Sanford (2012). Framed: America's 51 Constitutions and the Crisis of Governance. Oxford, New York: Oxford University Press. p. 234. ISBN 9780199890750. Archived from the original on October 10, 2018. Retrieved October 8, 2018. Accessed from Wikipedia, https://en.wikipedia.org/wiki/Mitch_McConnell#cite_note-:29-48)

McConnell has managed to sell the entire Republican party on the idea that monolithic party voting in the Senate will bring about desired results in the presidential election. He has used this idea to, in principle, incentivize and consolidate the views and attitudes of the Republican party as a whole, thus holding hostage anyone who may even attempt to dissent.

"McConnell has been able to establish a veritable assembly line for judicial confirmations" and *"while individual Republicans have at times complained privately about the majority leader, they have stood by the two of them on virtually every vote since the failure of Obamacare.* (Elving, NPR, 2019)

The Republicans who may not entirely agree with this particular approach and such an idea feel politically inclined to not stray, fearing it would, in essence, bring about political suicide as many believe it has for Republicans Jeb Bush, Jeffrey Flake, and Lynn Cheney.

Chapter Nine

"I've Fallen in Belief with Someone"

If one is still confused as to what the act of believing is, what it looks like, and how it's exercised, one need not look any further than to the experience one occupies while in a state of falling in love. Falling in love is deemed one of the most exhilarating experiences of being human. For some, finding love, falling in love, or maintaining a love affair has become life's main objective. People are so consumed with the idea of love they're willing to abandon and part with family, friends, religion, self-respect, and just about anything that stands to threaten this idea. People love to listen to music, watch romantic movies, and read romance novels, all to immerse themselves in this all-encompassing idea, surrendering themselves to its trials and tribulations over and over again. With such a huge emphasis put on love, people would be astounded to find out that the act of falling in love is less about love and more about belief. In essence, one actually falls into belief! Love on its face is nothing more than an inherent sentiment we're naturally inclined to feel toward any individual or thing we have come to identify with. This is a sentiment we share even with animals. In theory, real love for another person finds manifestation in the care and consideration you afford to that person's well-being. Relatively speaking, love is what you have given and received from your mother, father, brother, sister, children, or friends. It is an emotional responsibility you pledge to someone, regardless of the biological or emotional effect you receive or do not receive from it.

We fail to realize how much of a factor belief is in most of our relationships. We don't realize the reason we befriended the individual that ultimately betray our trust was because we "believed" that individual was not apt to betray us. But why? What would warrant us believing such an irrational idea? When one considers human nature and the inclinations we have to put our survival and self-interest first, what human being is not apt to betrayal? One of the reasons heartache is so painful is not so much due to the degree of love we possess for that person but is due to the "belief" we've attached to an idea we're intractably reluctant to compromise. We "believed" our significant other would never do anything disloyal or untrustworthy. But why? Again, what would warrant us giving anybody this type of belief? With so many people being products of impulse, who in the world is not capable of an indiscretion or an impulsive act? We should always hope that our significant others are not being dishonest, sexually promiscuous, or disloyal, but we should never believe it impossible to the point that we are emotionally overwhelmed and devastated if it happens. The degree of heartache one experiences during a breakup or divorce correlates directly to the degree of belief we had invested in it never being an actual possibility. There is no disappointment, torment, or pain comparable to the feeling of having something you believe and put your faith in turn out not to be what you anticipated—unless of course you never wholeheartedly believed in it from the start. This is the problem with romantic relationships and why the majority of us seem to always miss the mark. When one has found that significant other that inspires feelings of elation in us, this feeling is due to the unadulterated belief we're actively exercising about that individual. A belief in an idea of that person, as well as a reciprocal idea of that person's belief in us. It's pure belief that causes one to take joy in such a person: joy in how they look, how they walk, how they talk, how they dress, how they laugh, how they smile, joy in any of the most trivial things they may do. This experience is essentially a belief of a connection we have with this significant other. What makes the idea of a connection so significant is that, as human beings, we all seem to have this inherent sense of incompleteness we grapple with. As a result, we find ourselves in a constant state of searching for something, somebody, or anything to fill this void. Most of the time this search ends unsuccessfully, as we attempt to do so through our careers, possessions, and various amusements. Through history, the idea of a human connection seems to serve as close a remedy for this condition, as anything else available. This significant other provides for us an opportunity to believe in the idea that this void has finally been filled, hence we fall into belief. As individuals, each person's view of falling into belief (love) is relative to their own idiosyncratic ideas, subjectively requiring different variables for such an objective to be attained. For some, there is a stringent standard for those we consider able to bring about this state. This directly correlates with the conditions of the medieval period where the progressions and events leading up to a love affair was considered by many a noble event. Laura Ashe, an associate professor of English at Worcester College, Oxford, wrote about the climate during this period. Speaking here of 15th century Thomas Malory's *Le Morte Darthur*, she writes:

> "Malory's ideal of chivalry has love at its heart: 'thy quarrel must come of thy lady; he says, 'and such love I call virtuous love.' Each knight is to fight for the sake of his lady, with his victories he earns her love, and defends her honour. He is absolutely loyal to her and will follow her every command, whatever happens—whether she sends him on an impossible quest, banishes him from her company, or stands accused of some terrible crime, in desperate need of his help. Here, tragedy enters the picture. Lancelot's love of Guinevere can never have a happy ending, for she is King Arthur's queen. This is the epitome of 'courtly love' in literature: a commitment which binds the lovers until their deaths, but is never fulfilled in happy union. Lancelot's helpless devotion to Guinevere is dangerous, and it ultimately destroys the Court; gossips and slanderers tell the king of their affair, and Arthur is forced to take up arms against his greatest Knight." ("Love and Chivalry in the Middle Ages," Laura

Ashe, Jan. 31, 2018; https://www.bl.uk/medieval-literature/articles/love-and-chivalry-in-the-middle-ages)

The remnants of this medieval idea of proving oneself worthy of a companion's love continue to echo to the present day, as many men and women will indirectly require their partners to first earn their love through subjecting them to tough and undignified treatment before truly taking the relationship serious. Then there are some who are far less idealistic in matters of relationships, romance, and marriage, only seeing these things along the basis of practicality and a mere means to an end. These are usually the people who are more liberal in regard to the characteristics of a companion. Those with a more elaborate idea of love (belief), have a far higher standard for the partners they choose. For such people, they often fall into belief with people who appears to embody and personify the very ideas, whether physical or metaphysical, they've come to esteem and identify with, essentially idolizing what they deem to be the ideal idea! But usually the skewed perception of such individuals causes them to embellish their companion and the situation in a way that is not accurate; thus you have the term "love is blind." Again, for these people, the root behind this whole concept of love is actually belief. And what can be more gratifying to some than to live in the moment believing in such ideas with all of one's heart, even if it's not true and only just temporary.

But there's also a second premise as to why we're so infatuated with the experience of being in belief (love). And this happens when we find personal fulfillment as a result of having both our external and internal identity validated by someone we deem qualified and worthy enough to do it. Once again, "love" is not the keyword in this instant but rather "belief." In such a situation, our companion has either verified what we already believe to be true about our identity or inspired us to believe in an enhanced idea of ourselves much different and much more promising than the previous idea we held before. With this newfound perception of ourselves also comes a newfound satisfaction as well. But as emotionally basic and superficial as this may sound, not just anyone can bring about such possibilities in others, especially in matters of romance. As human beings, anyone we have yet to establish some degree of trust with, we're by nature cautious and suspicious of. For example, when you have two people courting one another, neither can definitively know what the general objective is of the other, as each partner may have their own ulterior motive for such a courtship. Because of this unknown, trust between two people is difficult and arduous to establish. So as a result, we tend not to trust the attempts of others to deliberately sway what it is we believe, suspicious of one's intentions. And usually the mere idea of someone even trying to change us, for what we deem to be their purpose, is often the root cause of many breakups in relationships. This may seem confusing because it seems to be the case with people we're in relationships with. But anyone else attempting to sway what we believe, is usually someone we already trust and expect to do so, such as family, close friends, and conventional norms. So it's rare for one to even allow a potential suitor the necessary degree of access and vulnerability possible to achieve such a task.

We now live in a time where people are flooded in feelings of inadequacy, so the validation provided through both forms of love (belief) is becoming increasingly relative to the low state people find themselves in. We now live in a time where people are suffering from a validation crisis. As we advance further into the future, everything seems to be growing at an exponential rate. And it seems that the more things grow, the smaller and more unimportant we all feel. The common individual in society is now becoming lost in the shuffle and apt to feel as though they are materially and immaterially worthless. This explains why social media is such a phenomenon because, theoretically, it serves as a means of shrinking our overgrowing community, society, and world into a more conceivable platform through which one can present themselves to be seen and heard, in a safe and self-fulfilling fashion. So anyone even remotely capable of inspiring another to believe something better about themselves, has accomplished a great and noble feat. Though this seems to be the more noble of the two, this particular experience of falling in belief (love) is apt to more adverse effects than the former. Because in most cases, when you validate another's sense of identity in a way that provides them happiness and a new-found belief, you become the incumbent presence necessary to sustain that person's happiness, because you're its cause. In some but not all cases, such individuals are often not able to believe such high spirited ideas that others inspire them to, thus rendering them dependents. So if it so happens that you're ever removed from the equation, you'd essentially take with you the ideas and the belief driving their happiness. So individuals who are recipients of such an experience tend to develop abandonment issues becoming clingy, needy, and sometimes even suicidal, in the advent that their loved one attempts or threatens to leave them.

Belief is such a potent phenomenon that there are people who become infatuated with merely employing its means with no intended ends at all. To wholeheartedly immerse one's belief into anything can be emotionally intoxicating in and of itself. This is the reason flattery is so appealing. In such situations, we may know a compliment or attention being lavished on us from a flatterer is usually exaggerated and disingenuous, but it's the joy the moment offers us to blindly believe that makes the whole experience so hypnotic, even if it's just a transient and superficial experience. But this fruitless experience of believing is also considered an inverse utilization of belief, bringing about adverse implications, because it's through this particular type of belief that deception as a whole is originally empowered and conceived into existence.

The belief we invest into ideas of love often bring along many adverse and subtle consequences that linger over extended periods of time. It's a common occurrence for lovers who part ways to continuously reminisce and romanticize relationships that were rather tumultuous, abusive, and toxic. Such individuals often presume that this continual contemplation of one's ex's is a result of the love or desire that still exists, when in some instances that is not the case. As one goes about believing in ideas of love, it sometimes happens we internalize these ideas to such an extent, that they attain consciousness, thus assimilating into our identity. This is a condition I call "Identity Overlap." We, in essence, internalize our lover to the point that we integrate them into our own personal identity. Such a condition causes much of our thinking to be binary to the point that we're thinking not just as ourselves but also as our lover as well. Or in other words, once you internalize another's identity into your own, at that point you stop thinking about that individual bilaterally and start thinking *as* that person unilaterally. This causes one to attribute certain thoughts, desires, impulses, and tendencies to that individual that may not be wholly accurate. This type of condition binds one to the lover to such an extent that every time you meditate about bettering yourself, you can't help but to also think about how to better that individual as well. It causes us to adore another on a much deeper level due to seeing them as an ideate version of ourselves. It may cause one to unconsciously dislike a complete stranger simply because they surmise that individual to be more compatible with their lover than they are. There are even rare cases where this condition causes one to subtly imagine that the lover is taking on characteristics of a parent or family member. This may be the cause of why many husbands indicate that after so long, their wives begin to remind them of their mothers. But oftentimes one of the primary concepts that brings about this condition is the idea of the "soul mate." The more belief we invest into the idea of another individual being our "soul mate," the more difficult it is to extricate and move on from that individual after the relationship runs its course. This social condition of identity overlap is not just limited to ex-lovers, but also parents, best friends, and many siblings are susceptible to this condition as well.

"When we invest our belief into something that ultimately turns out to be a lie, one has unwillingly been taken prisoner by that lie. It's actually one's belief that has been imprisoned. The actual lie or deception serves as the prison your held in and the idea or individual that created the deception, acts as the warden of that prison." ~ Swan

Chapter Ten
"Believing vs. Deceiving?"

Because of the power of this supernatural mechanism, our belief should not be exploited for any objective other than the purpose for which it was created otherwise the effects inevitably bring about adverse implications for the individual such as deception. Deception has no form, no purpose, and no existence until our inverse utilization of belief gives it realization. But ultimately, we give birth to the likelihood of deceit anytime we put our belief into anything unwarranted. Because many people, places and situations have the possibility of manifesting into something other than what we believe them to be, deception is always a possibility. So, the real search becomes one for anything worth believing in that does not bring with it the possibility of deception. This then precipitates the real question which is, is there anything or anybody in this world even capable of serving such a purpose. This is the universal question of existence one must reconcile for themselves. Until then we must settle for the administration of our belief with due diligence, otherwise we run the risk of being perpetually misled by anything and everything we encounter. One must understand, belief is not such that it should be placed in just anything or anyone. And for matters that do necessitate our belief, a safe and regulating level should be maintained to which one is keenly aware of when the proscribed boundaries are being breached. Because we've all believed in something, we all should understand where this boundary rests. The completion of such a task requires an effort of remaining conscious to one's own state of heart. There are natural matters of life that warrant our natural instruments of being and then there are supernatural matters of life that thus require our supernatural instruments of being, and believing is the only supernatural instrument of the human being I know of. Distinguishing between which matters are natural and supernatural lies the real test. Nonetheless, when we invest our supernatural belief into mere natural matters, deception is always one of the final results. The collateral impact of deception will always correlate to the degree of belief that is involved. The reason we consider "white lies" to be innocuous is these are instances where very little belief is brought into the equation. The more belief invested, the more dangerous the lie becomes, precipitating more catastrophic outcomes.

Like anything else, deceit is capable of taking on a life of its own. With enough momentum, it can acquire forms that seem to appear overwhelming in force. Most lies initially start off small and harmless. Harmless, because the matter may be so insignificant, no one ever invests any real belief into them, in which case they eventually die out. It is only when a lie is more or less believed by another or a number of individuals, that it then begins to evolve into something possessing life. When this happens, it's sustainability then becomes contingent on the amount of belief further invested into the lie. The more belief invested in it, the more commanding and truthful the lie appears. With enough belief, this lie could then become a reality in itself. If one ever embraces a lie, tuned reality, one's fate is then intertwined with the sustainment of that reality, which is inevitably destined to implode. The more the heart believes something to be true, only later to find out the opposite, the harder and the more painful the transition is out of this reality.

When we invest our belief into something that ultimately turns out to be a lie, one has unwillingly been taken prisoner by that lie. It's actually one's belief that has been imprisoned. The actual lie or deception serves as the prison you're held in and the idea or individual that created the deception, acts as the warden of that prison. This warden holds the exclusive power to either detain or release you from your captivity at any point in time. But being true to form, a warden rarely releases anybody from prison themselves because the warden's sole concern is the maintenance and occupation of the prison. And within any prison, it's actually the prisoners who maintain the day-to-day operations. It's the prisoners who prepare and serve the food, it's the prisoners who takes care of the institutional maintenance, who details the outside landscape to keep the prison looking up to par, and who provide the upkeep to ensure the facility is serviceable. So, the warden is in need of the prisoners because without them, the prison would cease to function. The same way the deceiver needs the belief that one entrusts to them, because in some way, shape or form that belief is serving and protecting their false sense of security: a sense of security they intend to maintain for as long as humanly possible. So, your warden, your liar, and your deceiver would never, by any means release you from the prison they've confined you to, because in doing so they would shatter their own illusionary reality they've fabricated and inhabited for themselves. But as you would find in a real prison setting, the real problem with people in prison is not one of rehabilitation, it's recidivism. A good majority of the prison population will eventually be let out of prison. In the same way that whoever is making you a prisoner to their lie will eventually be exposed. What's done in the dark will always come to the light. The problem with prisoners is after remaining incarcerated for so long they become susceptible to complacency, becoming content in their bondage. This causes the prisoner to subconsciously return to prison habitually. One of the leading factors contributing to the recidivism rate in America is due to inmates becoming institutionalized while in prison to the point that, when they're eventually let back out into society, they either refuse or are incapable of abandoning the prison temperament necessary while incarcerated. The same way the person in deceptive bondage opts to cope with it, unable to identify with anything else their presented with. Even when the lie is exposed and the prisoner is set free, this type of individual finds themselves vulnerable and unable to function without someone binding them to some false reality. These individuals feel as though the false reality provided by the liar is much safer than the unknown or even worst, becoming an emotional hitchhiker. So as a result, they often, by no coincidence, find themselves subjected to another warden, who places them in another emotional prison through the belief they willingly surrender. In essence, people are now being unconsciously conditioned to love the deception they are enraptured in.

Though on some level, we all must have some unconscious idea of how significant our belief is because most of us don't just willingly surrender it to any and everything. The more intelligent the person, the more protective and vigilant one is with their belief. But if not on a personal level, at the very least, we understand the significance of belief socially, which is demonstrated in how it's interpreted through criminal laws. For example, in Kentucky, there are three degrees of forgery listed in the Kentucky Revised Statutes. The first is,

> *Forgery in the 1st Degree. A person is guilty of forgery in the first degree when, with intent to defraud, deceive or injure another, he falsely makes...a written instrument which is or purports to be...(a) Part of an issue of money, stamps, securities or other valuable instruments issued by a government or governmental agency; or (b) Part of an issue of stock, bonds or other instruments representing interests in or claims against a corporate or other organization or its property.*

If one is found guilty of First Degree Forgery, the maximum penalty one can receive in prison is 10 years, but the minimum that one would serve is five years. In the subsection titled "Kentucky

Crime Commission/LRC Commentary," it justifies that the reason this offense is designated as *such is*

because this type of forgery impairs the public trust and confidence in governmental and corporate financial issues, a lack of public confidence in the validity of this type of instrument can have serious impact on governmental processes and the economy.

The second is forgery in the Second Degree.

A person is guilty of a forged in the second degree when, with intent to defraud, deceive or injure another, he falsely makes, completes or alters a written instrument or in the commission of a human trafficking offense...coerces another person to falsely make, complete or alter a written instrument, which is or purports to be...(a) A deed, will, codicil, contract, assignment, commercial instrument, credit card or other instrument which does or may evidence, create, transfer, terminate or otherwise affect a legal right, interest, obligation or status; or (b) A public record or an instrument filed or required or authorized by law to be filed in or with a public office or public employee; or (c) A written instrument officially issued or created by a public office, public employee or governmental agency.

If one is found guilty of Second Degree Forgery, the maximum penalty one can receive in prison is five years, but the minimum one would serve would be one year. In the subsection titled "Kentucky Crime Commission/LRC Commentary," it justifies that the reason this offense is designated as such is

> *"because of the increased potential harm to property interest and governmental functions. One is less likely to question public documents, and this lack of suspicion increases the likelihood of a successful fraud. In addition, the circulation of fraudulent records and recordable instruments tends to weaken public confidence in authentic records and governmental processes."*

The third is Forgery in the Third Degree.

> *"A person is guilty of forgery in the third degree when, with the intent to defraud, deceive, or injure another, he falsely makes, completes or alters a written instrument."*

If one is found guilty of Third Degree Forgery, the maximum penalty one can receive in jail is 12 months, but the minimum one would serve is 60 days. In the subsection titled "Kentucky Crime Commission/LRC Commentary," it justifies that the reason this offense is designated as such is,

> because the harm done is slight and because this grading permits misdemeanor dispositions of forgery charges.

What all three degrees of forgery have in common is the basis of deception that was perpetrated. The divergence in each degree is in the amount of damage brought about as result of each deception. What we define as damage in its various degrees also demonstrates what we as a society believe in most, as the law sets out to afford the severest penalty for instances with the severest damage. The first is the loss of stocks, bonds, stamps, securities, essentially money of any kind. If the loss of one's money is considered the most significant injury to be sustained, one can also imply that as a society, this is the idea we invest a substantial amount of belief in. Next comes ownership in the form of property, contracts, wills, or various financial instruments. And the last is cases where nothing deemed valuable is lost. To many it may seem that the punitive harshness inherent in each of the three degrees of forgery is ironically in keeping with the protection and interest of the wealthiest members of society, which very well may be the case. But we can naturally assume that our belief in a matter will always correlate with our interest in it. The belief I would put into the reliability of a bank that I was depositing just $20 of my money, would be far less than it would be if I were depositing say $20 million of my money. With this amount of money at stake, one would probably set out to know each and every one of the bank employees on a first-name basis.

In the commentary of the KRS, lawmakers acknowledge that, in totality, the impact of such offenses produces the impairment and weakness of public trust and confidence. In this context, both trust and confidence are being used in a way that denotes belief, which signifies the importance of our collective belief in certain ideas. The only way capitalism can sustain itself is if the citizens believe in the government's ability to regulate it. If banks could not rely on the government to protect it from criminals, the bank itself would not be deemed a reliable place to deposit money. If one could not believe in the reliability of the bank, no one would deposit their money there. If people were to stop putting their money in banks, there would be no way for banks to provide loans to entrepreneurs and businesses, which would then decrease business investment in general. With the decrease in new businesses, comes the loss of jobs, so on and so forth. So, belief plays a central role in the preservation of many functions of the government.

"Belief is the gasoline of the human spirit. As human beings, we are in constant need of something to believe in. It's our belief that drives us, moves us, inspires us and influences us." ~ Swan

Chapter Eleven
"Believing with Inspiration"

Up until this point, belief has been referenced here as the practical means through which we materialize intangible ideas into either physical or meta-physical phenomena. But this is just one of the many features of belief. We are also able to exploit belief for purposes of inspiration. Unbeknown to most people, inspiration is one of the most gratifying and sought after sensations of the heart. As humans we are emotional beings, created to navigate the world through the prism of feeling. It's our belief that provides identity and color to our feelings in a way that is capable of vitalizing or devitalizing life for each individual. For the conscious human being, there is nothing more emotionally fulfilling than to have a cause one wholeheartedly believes in. This cause may be as noble as ending world hunger or as humble as parenting one's own children. The causes we take up are not limited in scope, but only in the belief we invest in them. Without such, life becomes a bland existence of routine day to day normalities. It's the belief we apply to our approach to life, that changes ordinary and minor undertakings, into noble and motivating life purposes worthy of our sacrifice. When we are oblivious to the true significance of our capacity to believe, this limits our ability to influence and understand why we're affected by certain experiences. In most cases, we cannot control certain experiences we encounter in life, we do however have the power to change how we identify with those experiences, by simply injecting our belief into these matters in a way that validates our personal identity as individuals. For example, consider a woman working as a Certified Nurse's Assistant at a nursing home. For her, coming to work every day, having to deal with the stresses of a nursing home can be draining and emotionally unfulfilling. She first deals with staff and scheduling discrepancies, as the turnover rate at such jobs is extremely high. Because of such, there are days when there are not enough nurses to tend to the usual overcrowding demands of patients. This results in her being assigned to tend to more patients than due diligence would normally call for, naturally interfering with the necessary quality of care entitled to each patient. In tending to these patients, she often deals with those who are uncooperative, senile, belligerent, and physically and sometimes sexually aggressive. On top of this, she may have to also deal with the usual politics of the workplace, such as incompetent management, unprofessional bosses, ill-mannered coworkers, and unhealthy working conditions. After a while, the job under those conditions gives this woman nothing to believe in that would inspire her in any way. Such situations at work usually spill over into one's emotional well-being after leaving work, contributing to a life of insipidness and depression. But if by chance, she can change her belief about this job, she could change everything.

For example, say this woman begins ruminating about her life and how "The Reality" will judge her when it's over. And because the majority of her life will be spent working at this job, this leads her to conceive of the idea that the basis of how she'll be judged when she dies will be on her job performance or lack thereof. If this idea were actually internalized, this woman's job would now look very differently than it had before. Her belief has now inspired her and equipped her with clarity of purpose, sincerity, and devotion. As a result of the belief in this idea, she now comes to work with a more positive attitude in general. This leads her to a better disposition and better communication with her coworkers. Her newfound sincerity has now inspired her to not just care for her patients with work formality, seeing them as strangers she has no personal regard for, but now seeing them in the same light of compassion she would her own relatives. This causes her to interact with each patient with empathy, now treating them as the human beings everyone else tends to forget they are. This causes her patients to love her and see her as more than just a nurse, causing them to respond to her more favorably than others. Her devotion to the task at hand, now inspires her to be more personally invested in the overall function of the nursing home, rather than being indifferent to its affairs after her shift has ended. As a result of being more invested, her interest becomes one with management causing her to now take extra initiative, introduce innovative ideas, solve problems, and make useful suggestions, all to the betterment of the nursing home. Eventually this is recognized by management, winning her their respect and confidence, which leads to an increase of responsibility and higher job title. The increase in responsibility and job title brings with it promotions and advancements. But even if by some irregularity, events don't unfold this way, the mere change of belief with all of its positive effects, is capable of doing so much for the well-being of a woman in such situations. Our belief is the only thing standing in the way of the inspiration necessary to surmount and exceed life's obstacles.

Belief is the gasoline of the human spirit. As human beings, we are in constant need of something to believe in. It's our belief that drives us, moves us, inspires us, and influences us. You show me an individual with nothing to believe in, and I'll show you an individual with no motivation to get out of bed in the morning, an individual with no genuine love or concern for the people in their lives, an individual with no interest in their own personal growth and an individual with absolutely nothing to offer the world. These types of individuals suffer from feelings of powerlessness and often become suicidal due to the lack of inspiration in life. Never realizing that it is they themselves who have abandoned the only instrument through which to change their hopeless condition, belief. We've been graciously enabled with the power to be creators of the world at large, but to a greater extent, our own individual world. The individual world only you occupy, relative to any and everything encompassing your life. In this world you are the deity responsible for creating the Sun, air, moon, and stars. And the tool through which we construct our world is our very belief. The ideas we invest our belief in form the basis of all of our aspirations, preferences, sense of securities, gratifications, and overall well-being. Anytime someone initiates a romantic relationship with another individual thought to be of lower status whether it be from a physical, social, or financial standpoint, this is usually due to the initiator being someone who is not subject to common conventions, but rather someone who has developed and acted on their own personal ideas through belief. If there were no one in the world to act on their own belief, no one would deviate from what is typical and expected, making life bland and monotonous. Anytime you a hear a story about someone from humble beginnings making something of themselves, someone beating the odds to become a success story, or someone having gone through insurmountable adversity only to finally reach their objective, it is due to them refusing to merely believe in the negative ideas relative to their identity. Instead, such individuals apply their belief to their own self-made ideas thus dictating the situation at hand. These individuals ultimately become the difference makers in the world. These are the people that stand out eventually becoming pioneers we all rely on for direction in various matters. The elaborate ideal system they've constructed for themselves provides them self-assurance to undertake what others deem to be impossible. These individuals have made the conscious decision to serve as the sole proprietors of their ideal systems, thus making them the sole architects of their world and leaders of the world at large.

As these individuals audaciously exercise their belief, willfully assuming who they elect to be, rather than who life makes them. They are able to remove and avoid the many obstacles they come across, thereby attaining to heights unknown to most, while everyone around such individuals is left basking in the ambiance of their triumphs. The belief exercised by these individuals has progressive implications for everything and everyone affected by it but even more so for those who witness it firsthand. This may be the reason that the companions and confidants of anyone who reaches a state of distinction oftentimes are also brought to a respective level of distinction in their own right. Even after the master passes away, their students remain elevated, having experienced and internalized the master's presence and aura. This being the case because the belief of the believer is so empowering and infectious, it naturally inspires and liberates everyone else to utilize their belief as well.

Chapter Twelve
"Consciousness Malfunction—The New Name for Mental Health"

Most of the ideas we come to believe in throughout our lives are embraced unconsciously, without much reflection or reasoning to their implications. When one unconsciously believes in an idea, the underlying principle behind such ideas usually happens to be those we already in nature incline toward, identify with, or approve of. For example, the phrase "Black Lives Matter" was a polarizing term during the year 2020, as police brutality was highlighted in America. In opposition to such protests, this prompted people to counter-protest using the term "Blue Lives Matter" which invalidated the issue and redirected it to police safety instead. These two phrases or in this case ideas, sparked somewhat of a divide between two distinct groups of people in America. In most cases, the people who supported the expression "black lives matter" were usually people who were already liberal or Democrat, had previously felt that police brutality was a problem, and had already felt that race relations was a major problem in the country, while those less inclined or outright indifferent to the phrase were usually individuals who were beforehand Republicans or conservatives, had already felt that police brutality was exaggerated or not a problem at all, and who may have already held some racist views toward minorities and felt no change was needed. Another example is, if you find that you come from a wealthy family, you are conservative about issues such as immigration, public assistance, and you favor tax cuts for the wealthy and harsher drug laws for low level offenders, it's not unrealistic to presume that you may have embraced a negative or stereotypical idea about poor minorities at some point in your development of growth. Day in and day out we are constantly investing into ideas that will significantly impact the course of our entire lives without us ever realizing it. The only means we have at our disposal to fend off unconsciously believing in venomous ideas is to consistently maintain an awareness of our inner self. This means to familiarize oneself with the state of one's consciousness. We tell children when they're young to believe in themselves, but we neglect to tell them how exactly to do so. We neglect to teach them this concept is not just limited to believing you are capable of some achievement. We neglect to teach them that believing in oneself denotes believing in the power inherent in each of us; a power that we must take initiative to realize, understand, preserve, and exercise. When we become adept at such a process, we will immediately sense the true essence of the ideas we encounter and how susceptible we are to their internalization. The majority of those who suffer from what society deems mental health problems, are those not aware of their state of heart and who do not fully consider and evaluate the ideas they embrace. Through their obliviousness, they allow themselves to believe and internalize destructive ideas which compromise their opportunities and identities. Or in other words, they allow such ideas free penetration into their consciousness with little to no resistance. For many, this happens as a result of habit, as our daily lives become more and more commonplace. As we maneuver through our affairs routinely, doing the same things over and over again, we eventually reach a point where we're doing just about everything absentmindedly. And when most of the things we do becomes routine, we are apt to find ourselves no longer operating from a state of heart, but rather one of second nature or unconsciousness. In an unconscious state, one becomes mechanical in their approach to life in a way that limits all perception and reason. Without these two security blankets, the consciousness is left abandoned and unoccupied with no protection from outside intrusion. Because of this obliviousness we have towards our inner dimension, there are individuals who spend most of their lives in unconscious reality. The individual who lacks any type of spiritual depth and goes through life routinely can easily reach a state that they eat unconsciously, converse unconsciously, drive unconsciously, cook unconsciously, have sex unconsciously, exercise unconsciously, etc. As our society modernizes, the impact of such an atmosphere is becoming detrimental to the essence of the human being. As a result, activities we deem to be ordinary such as watching movies, television shows, and news stations, reading tabloid magazines and newspapers, and listening to music have all become the cradles of some of our most rigid and irrational ideas. People are no longer watching the news networks for investigative reporting but more so to feed into propaganda that will reinforce and strengthen the basis of their identity. The movie industry has now taken it upon themselves to educate or rather unconsciously manipulate the public through movies that seem to consistently designate who the antagonist are, what the heroes should look like, and setting the standard for what the prevailing norms should be. People seem to lose themselves in these ordinary activities presuming they are harmless, all the while oblivious to the real effect taking place under the surface on an emotional, intellectual, and spiritual level. As a result of this stimuli-infested society, we are now subconsciously internalizing such a wide array of ideas, at such a prolific rate, our identities are being compromised as a result of consciousness overload. Everywhere you look, you'll find stimuli loaded with subtle and covert messages forcefully grabbing our attention. In the past, the best example of this was television, as commercials, movies, and sitcoms were all laced with images that affected people subconsciously. But social media has now officially taken over this role, encompassing anything and everything within society. Social media has now become the number one source for dissemination of widespread images, in a much more efficient manner than television ever could. Social media has now also become the main source of influence for the greater majority in our society and perhaps even the world. And because social media provides a platform through which people from all across the world can communicate, exchange, and share ideas, it is also now the number one source of propaganda. When one factors the growing phenomenon of social networking, along with how much of our time is spent online, it explains why people's consciousness have begun to breakdown.

"The use of Facebook and social media has grown tremendously over the past ten years. Most people who use the internet utilizes social media: 95% of all teens (13-17) are online; 81% of online teens frequent some type of social media, up from 55% of online teens in 2006; 77% of online teens use Facebook; 74% of adult internet users use social media, compared to just 8% ten years

ago. The time people spend on social media is substantial. An estimated 28% of all time spent online is spent on social networking; 22% of teens log on to a social media site more than 10 times a day, and more than half of adolescents log on to a social media site more than once a day. In 2014 Facebook estimated that the average user spends 8.3 hours a month on the site.

Conversely, a number of studies emphasize the potentially, negative consequences of sites like Facebook. They document the incidence of anxiety, depression, ADHD, eating disorders and addiction among users." ("Facebook and Mental Health: Is Social Media Hurting or Helping? https://www.mentalhelp.net/internet/social-media-hurting-or-helping)

The effect such an expansive outlet of stimuli has on society's mental health is demonstrated in an article written by Shawn Lim, Excessive Use of Facebook Could Trigger Depression, Study Finds," for *The Drum*.

"People who spend most of their time on Facebook are at higher risk of suffering from depression. This is according to a study by

Singapore's Nanyang Technological University which also found the more people use Facebook, the higher the levels of envy, which led to feelings or depression. 'Social rank theory says we engage in social comparison, which is something we cannot escape because it's how we make sense of our own social identity. But this process of comparison can lead us to feeling down when we see someone having more resources than we do,' said associate professor Edson C Tandoc Jr, from the NTU Centre for Information Integrity and the Internet....When [participants] indicated they were feeling envious, there was a stronger relationship between Facebook use and signs of depression." (https://www.thedrum.com/news/2021/08/16/excessive-use-facebook-could-trigger-depression-study-finds)

This illustrates how as a society; we now deem social media to be the status quo. So everything we see on social media serves as an idea we often believe, thus leading to the ultimate pursuit of its actualization, even in cases where actualization of such ideas is an anomaly. We see this on TikTok with millions of people creating videos to emulate something they've seen someone else do.

With social media so infused in our ordinary affairs, it's unlikely and impractical that one will spontaneously remove oneself from such an outlet. But at the very least, one must consider the implications of overexposure and manage one's exposure through the regulation of belief. If one can remain aware of their own state of heart while carrying out our common day to day affairs, one can then filter every notion, impression, and idea attempting to subtly pass through our consciousness unnoticed. The irony with the human heart is it's much easier to unconsciously attach your heart to an idea to your detriment than it is to willfully internalize one to your benefit. So before you can build a healthy ideal system that suits your purpose, one should determine if your current identity has been adversely affected through lapses of such belief.

Our identities are a direct product of the ideas we allow to segue into our consciousness, so once the consciousness begins to malfunction as a result of over-influx, it can only bring about a malfunction of identity in the process, thus leading to widespread mental health problems or more accurately, consciousness malfunction problems. The theory of Cognitive Dissonance created by Leon Festinger is an existing concept very similar to the theory of Consciousness Malfunction presented here but is different for a number of reasons. Leon Festinger essentially theorized that in Cognitive Dissonance,

> *"People hold many different cognitions about their world, e.g., about their environment and their personalities....In an event wherein some of these cognitions clash, an unsettling state of tension occurs...."* ("Cognitive Dissonance Experiment," https://explorable.com/cognitive-dissonance-experiment)

One of the key differences between the two concepts specifically is that Fastinger also suggests

> "every person has innate drives to keep all his cognitions in a harmonious state and avoid a state of tension or dissonance. If a person encounters a state of dissonance, the discomfort brought by the conflict of cognition leads to an alteration in one of the involved cognitions to reduce the conflict and bring a harmonious state once again."

So the common basis that brings about both these particular theories is in fact, idea incompatibility. Idea incompatibility is a widely recognized concept studied and treated both in psychiatry and psychology. I opine that the lack of an adequate remedy to this condition is the result of professionals in both fields placing more emphasis on the behavior that is brought about through the *emotional dilemma* of conflicting ideas, which in light of cognitive dissonance being touted and highly validated in both fields, is illogical because of the fact that it's purported to be a self-correcting phenomenon, by way of any effect coming as a result of dissonance, as Festinger suggests above, being innately brought back into consonance and harmony instinctually.

Consciousness Malfunction takes into account the true nature of belief; the various processes through which ideas are conceived, nourished, and empowered, and internalized; as well as the true foundation and locale of one's identity within the heart. So because our supernatural belief precludes the gathering of experimental data, testing of theories using data and developing models that match the data, Consciousness Malfunction can never be appreciated in its true light. The DSM (Diagnostic Statistical manual) does not take into account the various degrees a cognition undergoes before its realization, so how could it even attempt to go about developing an adequate treatment? Festinger, being the creator of cognitive dissonance, does not address the different measures it takes to bring an idea from a state of cognition to one of causation. As redundant as this may seem, this is vitally important because as human beings we don't necessarily act on every idea we're consciously susceptible to and we're not just vulnerably susceptible to every idea we act on. Many examples of cognitive dissonance merely entail instances of individuals on the brink of a moral dilemma resulting from some matter they find difficult to emotionally process. As a matter of fact, Cognitive Dissonance may actually be the prelude to in-belief! But getting back to the topic, by societal standards, not just anybody who is susceptible to conflicting ideas is considered mentally unstable; and this is because, everybody is essentially prone to conflicting ideas. And such *emotional dilemmas* do not routinely bring about fragmented identities. There's a difference between merely acting on an idea versus internalizing an idea. I'm in no way implying that incompatible ideas, psychoses, and personality disorders are new symptoms that originated through Consciousness Malfunction. What I am positing is that because Consciousness Malfunction is explained in the true context through which one systematically internalizes ideas into realization, it separates itself from other diagnoses. In my opinion, many medically recognized disorders do not pinpoint actual disorders but rather serve as further supererogatory descriptions of the underlying symptom. This is tantamount to us naming cancer, "The Tumor" and then going on and on about the tumor, such as the size of the tumor, how the tumor behaves, and how fatal the tumor is. If one doesn't identify or address the abnormal cell division behind the malignant growth of the tumor, how could there ever be the hope of a cure?

As humans, we've been given the power to fashion ourselves how we see fit, but with any power comes responsibility. As we go about the process of molding ourselves, we must do so with the upmost due diligence because the mismanagement of such an undertaking could spell long-term disaster for the architect. The same way the scientist studies biological and chemical processes, one must first come to understand the science and nature of ideas. It's imperative that one knows how ideas act, react, and interact to other ideas as such ideas may eventually become the idea we internalize into our general identity. Due to our lack of appreciation of the true essence of ideas and the existence we give them through belief, people are oblivious to how easy we all are subject to such lapses of consciousness. Ideas are no different from organisms in that, once they attain consciousness they essentially take on a life of their own. And when this happens, it's possible that certain ideas are liable to take us to places and into situations we would much rather not venture. For example, if one were to believe in ideas of extreme patriotism for their country, and simultaneously, believe in ideas that this same country is disingenuous with its citizens regarding domestic affairs, it could bring about not just conflicting ideas, but conflicting identities leading to conflicting realities as we see with Consciousness Malfunction. When these two ideas attain consciousness, this individual, as Festinger theorized, will attempt to harmonize these realities by doing something he thinks will reconcile and appease both, thereby carrying out what he deems to be patriotic sacrifice, that in reality renders him a treasonist to the very country he claims to be a martyr for. This demonstrates that such an act does not actually harmonize this dissonance but serves as a further indication of one's reality/identity/idea undergoing a state of malfunction.

We all experience conflicting thoughts about many things in life. One of the most important ideas relative to human beings also happens to be probably the most cognitive dissonant idea a person can have, which is the existence of "God." Does not a belief in an All-powerful "God" that asserts to hear all and see all but is yet invisible to our physical eyesight and mute to our audible hearing, an instance of two conflicting ideas? Could not one then be inclined to presume that the notion of Jesus Christ being God incarnated is actually a product of New Testament writer Paul trying to harmonize his cognitive dissonance about the existence of God? These are just a couple of the many concepts people are typically conflicted with but unless such ideas are believed and manifested into either a subjective, unconscious, conscious, terrestrial, ideate or spiritual reality; they generally bear no significant consequence to the individual's state of consciousness.

The theoretical treatment for Consciousness Malfunction begins first and foremost with Realization. For those who have reached this condition unconsciously, realization is probably the most important part of the treatment. But this is probably the most difficult to come to terms with because this is essentially acknowledgment. And acknowledgment of a disorder involving our own inner self requires a state of objectivity and humility, something many in our society are handicapped from.

What makes such an acknowledgment so difficult is that it hints at our incompetence in managing the one thing that everyone should be capable of managing, the self. The stigma of losing one's sanity is probably one of the most frowned-upon stigmas in society. People are so averse to this stigma they'd go to the furthest extremes— extremes that even make them look crazy, just to prove they're not crazy. Denial is one of the common inhibitors to any mode of progress. There have been many patients, who in pride, would not acknowledge their sickness unfortunately precluding their treatment. If there is no acknowledgment of a problem, there exists no seeking of a solution. When we get to a point that we can acknowledge this, the next step is to then direct the treatment to the manner of one's belief. When we suffer from conditions that are belief oriented, the treatment, if to be effective can only be belief oriented. And how could there have been such a treatment when no one has accurately systemized this process until now?

Anytime one embraces a detrimental idea that does not bring about an actual condition, one can rectify the matter by dismantling the detrimental idea. But in cases involving Consciousness Malfunction, one has to then begin the process of de-believing in an idea or ideas that are bringing about this malfunctioning condition. The difficulty of this process of de-believing depends on the number of ideas, causing the condition. The process of de-believing an idea or ideas entails one utilizing the second set of 3'R's, which also correlate with the first set from chapter one. These 3'R's are Reconciling, Resigning, and Relinquishing.

These 3 R's have to be used as a guide through the de-believing process. Step one: To reconcile both ideas to one's overall identity, because the malfunction one experiences is not a product of the consciousness itself, but rather from the commotion of the ideas within it. These conflicting ideas in one's consciousness are symbolically acting as rams that are continuously head-butting one another over and over again. These in actuality, are the two ideas attempting to reconcile their conflict through forceful means. So one has to first reconcile each idea to one's identity to bring about a temporary truce. This reconciliation consists of *Remembering* why and how these ideas were initially embraced. In the context of believing, this is the process of conceptualizing and cultivating the idea to its full form. Step two: To resign the idea from its position. The establishment of a temporary truce between the two conflicting ideas was not the objective but was rather a stall tactic. Though one has brought about a truce, this treaty will not last. The conflict will reemerge at any point in time that either of the ideas is stimulated. I explained this in chapter one by describing how our ideas are like "active entities within themselves." So for this reason, both of these ideas have to be relieved of their duties to repair the malfunctioning one is experiencing. The process of Resigning the ideas from their position involves us to *Reason* how these ideas are no longer useful to our purpose and who we're striving to be. In the context of Believing, this is where we empower our idea with its potency. Step Three: To Relinquish the idea from our consciousness. If we've empowered the idea enough through our Reasoning of its uselessness, we will then have the power to remove it completely from our identity. We finalize the process through *Ridiculing* the idea to ourselves in a way that it seems repugnant to us. This causes us over time to unconsciously disassociate ourselves from its stimuli in our reality. In the context of belief, this is the final stage of internalization. For any type of physician to assist someone through this is rare and challenging due to the nature of belief and it being a capacity that is uniquely insulated in a way that is physically and materially inaccessible to others. And for the individuals who are content in a state of Consciousness Malfunction and who have attained this state as a result of their own conscious doing, the treatment for such individuals is a waste of time. Such individuals will superficially seek treatment for their conditions while concealing the true cause of their inability to be rehabilitated from this state of malfunction.

The reason mental health has reached such a degree it has is due to there being no viable treatment to cure it. Doctors are prescribing anti-depressant pills in high volume, which do nothing but lead to addiction. Psychiatrists and psychologist provide no solution to this problem other than offering people various coping mechanisms to employ. And therapy is limited to the same outdated psychoanalysis treatment that has not proved effective in the least. We fail in our ability to remedy this problem because we neglect the most important aspect in terms of treatment, which is identifying where the illness is located. More specifically, we have not pinpointed exactly where the illness is emanating from. For if one does not know what part of the body an illness is attacking, how can one know where to direct the treatment? The name "mental health" itself demonstrates the root of this fundamental fallacy. As mentioned in the earlier chapter, the brain is not the source of our radial awareness of being. It's not from the brain that we intellectually perceive, reason, understand, and exist. Our essence is not located in the upper regions of the human body as presumed but in the heart. The correct identification of where these mental health diseases are transpiring, makes up a good portion of the treatment needed to cure it. Oddly enough, the mere misidentification of the true self has brought about much of this mental health crisis in its own right. One of the trademark symptoms of someone suffering from a mental health disorder is that they cannot stop or tune out the voices in their head. There are countless people who commit horrific acts only to later attribute them to some voice in their head prompting them to do so. For example, some of the common symptoms of schizophrenia are (1) confusing thought patterns; thoughts and speech become a form of self-expression rather than of communication; (2) inappropriate emotional responses, varying from apathy to happiness or rage; (3) hallucinations: the perceiving of mental images as sensory perceptions (hearing voices, having visions, Imagining smells, and the like; and (4) delusions: misinterpretations of reality, such as perceiving nonexistent threats or feeling all-powerful. Just as many other mental health disorders are generally associated with the brain, disorders such as anxiety disorder, depression, bipolar disorder, obsessive-compulsive disorder, post-traumatic stress disorder, personality disorder, eating disorder and attention deficient/hyperactive disorder (ADHD). Many of these disorders are diagnosed as being oriented or derived from one's "thoughts" implicating the source of the disorder being of the mind. In light of this prevailing idea, It's safe to say that we as a society have internalized this idea of "Psyche Disorientation." Because of our general misidentification of the true self of the human being, people are wholeheartedly orienting and projecting their true essence to somewhere in the body it's actually not stationed.

This is no different than if we determined that our hands were made to walk on, the feet to grasp with, the ears to smell with and the nose to hear with. Society has indoctrinated this idea into everyone to the extent of internalization. The reason the imagination leads people to the idea that they're hearing voices in their head is because we've all been led to presume that our thinking is a product of the brain. When in actuality the only activity occurring in the brain is the movement of biological neurons, sending electrical impulses throughout our body to activate various functions of the body. So neither thought, awareness, nor intellectual perception are experienced in the same location their biological processes are stimulated from. This is one of the reasons that meditation and yoga have always been so highly suggested for mental health illnesses, because such practices involve quieting the mind. When in all logic, the idea of quieting the mind should actually signify to people the absence of activity "in the mind" from the onset. These practices should only be used as a guide to reach this conclusion, otherwise the practice serves no remedial purpose. This act of meditation endorsed by mental health physicians is a process that entails keeping the body completely still as a means of ceasing mental thought. In essence, this would imply that the best treatment for these thought oriented disorders is to not think or use the brain at all. Something that is essentially impossible nor necessary. Sleep is not even a means of resting the brain, as the brain is essentially more active in sleep as it is during the waking hours. For the brain was not constructed to cease activity, and in the event that it ever does, this would also cease one's life as well. Another treatment suggested for many disorders is cerebrally being in the now or remaining in the present moment, which is also an initiative to get out of one's own head or thoughts. Something that humans cannot afford to do, not even for a second. Thinking, when performed in its correct capacity, is just as essential for our optimal functioning as the engine is to the automobile. But improperly orienting the act of thinking to the head has brought about imaginary effects, necessitating imaginary treatments. Our indoctrinating the public through various means, that thinking is a brain-oriented process, is an idea we have all collectively internalized to our own detriment. Going forward we must extricate ourselves, from such mistaken concepts. We must realize that even something as natural as thinking must first be put into the right perspective and adequately developed because erroneous thinking can only lead to consciousness malfunction.

In conclusion, the sole mechanism of the incorporeal heart of the human being is to believe. The heart has various functions but only one real mechanism. We may presume that we're exercising a variety of tools through the heart but essentially all we're really doing is, believing. If our inner heart were a game system, our belief would be its remote controller. To some degree, we all naturally exercise belief but the effects are not the same when one is not consciously exercising it with intellect. The effects are not the same when one is not exercising it as naturally intended. The effects are not the same if one doesn't know its true nature. Our belief is a supernatural process with the exclusive capacity to network with our supernatural heart. The ultimate end to which we should facilitate our heart is a subjective question no self-help book should or could help you to determine. How one chooses to exercise this extraterrestrial apparatus will essentially determine how one is held accountable in a much higher Reality of existence. The purpose of this book is not to proclaim, declare, or warn about the inevitable, for that reason, various religions, prophets and disciples have been manifested. The purpose of this book is merely to outline and possibly inspire the true nature, function, and purpose behind our power. Whether you *believe* it or *in-believe* is up to you.

www.ingramcontent.com/pod-product-compliance
Lightning Source LLC
Chambersburg PA
CBHW062213270326
41930CB00009B/1721